The Railroad and the CANYON

Also by Rudy J. Gerber:

Grand Canyon Railroad: Illustrated Guidebook
(Primer Publishers, Phoenix)

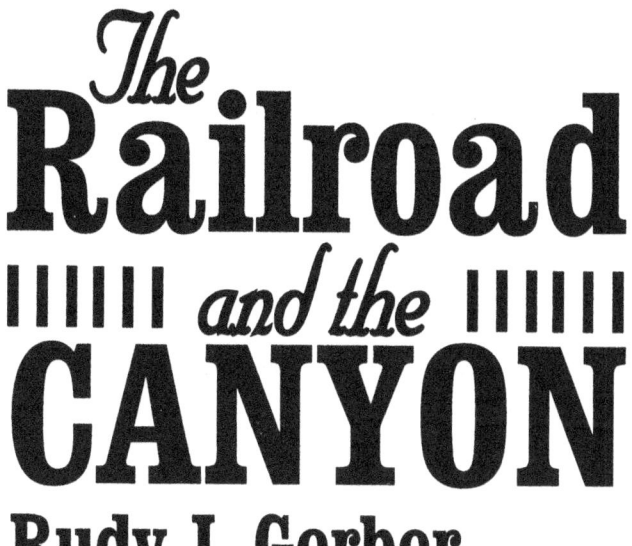

The Railroad and the Canyon

Rudy J. Gerber

A FIREBIRD PRESS BOOK

PELICAN PUBLISHING COMPANY
Gretna 1998

Copyright © 1995
By Rudy J. Gerber
All rights reserved

To Jennifer Anne Gerber, my daughter—
grand as the Canyon

The word "Pelican" and the depiction of a pelican are trademarks
of Pelican Publishing Company, Inc.,
and are registered in the U.S. Patent and Trademark Office.

Library of Congress Cataloging-in-Publication Data

Gerber, Rudy J.
    The railroad and the canyon / Rudy J. Gerber.
    p. cm.
    ISBN 0-88289-986-4
    1. Grand Canyon (Ariz.)—History. 2. Railroads—Arizona—Grand
Canyon Region—History. 3. Tourist trade—Arizona—Grand Canyon
Region—History. I. Title.
F788.G43 1994
979.1'32—dc20   93-50208
                                                                                    CIP

Manufactured in the United States of America
Published by Pelican Publishing Company, Inc.
1000 Burmaster Street, Gretna, Louisiana 70053

Contents

            Acknowledgments   7
            Introduction   9
Chapter 1   Distant Beginnings   13
Chapter 2   Stagecoaches to the Canyon   27
Chapter 3   First Rails to the Rim   41
Chapter 4   Civilizing the Frontier at Williams and the Canyon   53
Chapter 5   Travel Promotions   69
Chapter 6   Mary Jane Colter and Canyon Architecture   81
Chapter 7   End of the Line   97
Chapter 8   Re-inaugurating the Rails   101
Chapter 9   History and Archeology en Route   109
            Epilogue   127

Acknowledgments

I wish to thank Teri Cleeland and Larry Lesko of the Kaibab National Forest for archeological assistance. Along with the Grand Canyon, indeed even more than the canyon, my daughter Jennifer inspired these pages. She and the Canyon remind me of a medieval song to the Virgin that could be sung for all three:

Tota pulchra es
Et macula non est in te
Quam speciosa, quam suavis
In deliciis conceptio illibata.
Veni, veni, veni Magno,
Veni coram aderis.

How beautiful are you,
Without any stain,
How serene, how fair
In all your wondrous beginnings.
Come, come, come Beautiful One,
Come and be with us.

Introduction

"God made the Canyon and John Hance made its trails"—such was railroader Buckey O'Neill's curt summary of all Grand Canyon history. Much more lies between the lines. If God made the Canyon and Hance made its trails, most of the rest of its early human history came from the Santa Fe and Grand Canyon railways. In some form, the railroad shaped the beginning of its human development. Even before the arrival of the rails, railroad fever sponsored most of the early expeditions, explorations, and stage lines toward the Canyon.

Much of the Canyon's original challenge had to do with these explorations. Its first discoverers saw it as a vast barrier. They described it in forbidding terms—a grave, barrier, a prison. The Havasupai Indians called it *Wikatata,* or "Rough Rim." The Hopis saw it as the place of entry and exit from the underworld. Coronado's historian Castenada described it as *barranca,* a "forbidding canyon." Father Garces, the first white man to name it, called it a "prison." Engineer Stanton, who tried to build a railroad through it, called it "death canyon." Powell, who navigated it, called it "our granite prison," and Ives, who charted it, termed it the "gate of hell."

This barrier remained unexplored for a long time. From 1540 to the mid-1800s, no white man except Father Garces came to its rims. Its exploration only began in the mid-nineteenth century when Washington contemplated a transcontinental railroad running from the Midwest to California. Early Canyon explorations accordingly parallel surveys for this western railroad, for the railroad was seen as the principal way to confront this barrier to western expansion.

The Santa Fe Railway first arrived sixty miles south of the Canyon in 1882 under the name "Atlantic and Pacific." It soon spawned stagecoaches to the rim. One of the first stage stops—Red Horse station—became one of the Canyon's first hotels and later its post office.

After its arrival at the rim in 1901, the railroad constructed elegant hotel and station facilities. Working with the Fred Harvey Company and the National Park Service, the Santa Fe fostered unique architectural development at the south rim that spanned half a century over a distance of some one hundred miles. El Tovar, Bright Angel Lodge, the Watchtower, Phantom Ranch, Hopi House, Hermit's Rest, the Lookout, and Buckey O'Neill's cabin, as well as the Hermit Trail and even the Hance Trail, have their roots intertwined in the railroad. And this history is not all a matter of the past: the rails to the Canyon still ring with trains almost a century later.

The interplay between the railroad and the Canyon offers an inviting and little-told piece of western history, whose message is human confrontation with an awesome barrier—a barrier approached, enhanced, preserved, and celebrated but not surmounted. This is the story of that interplay.

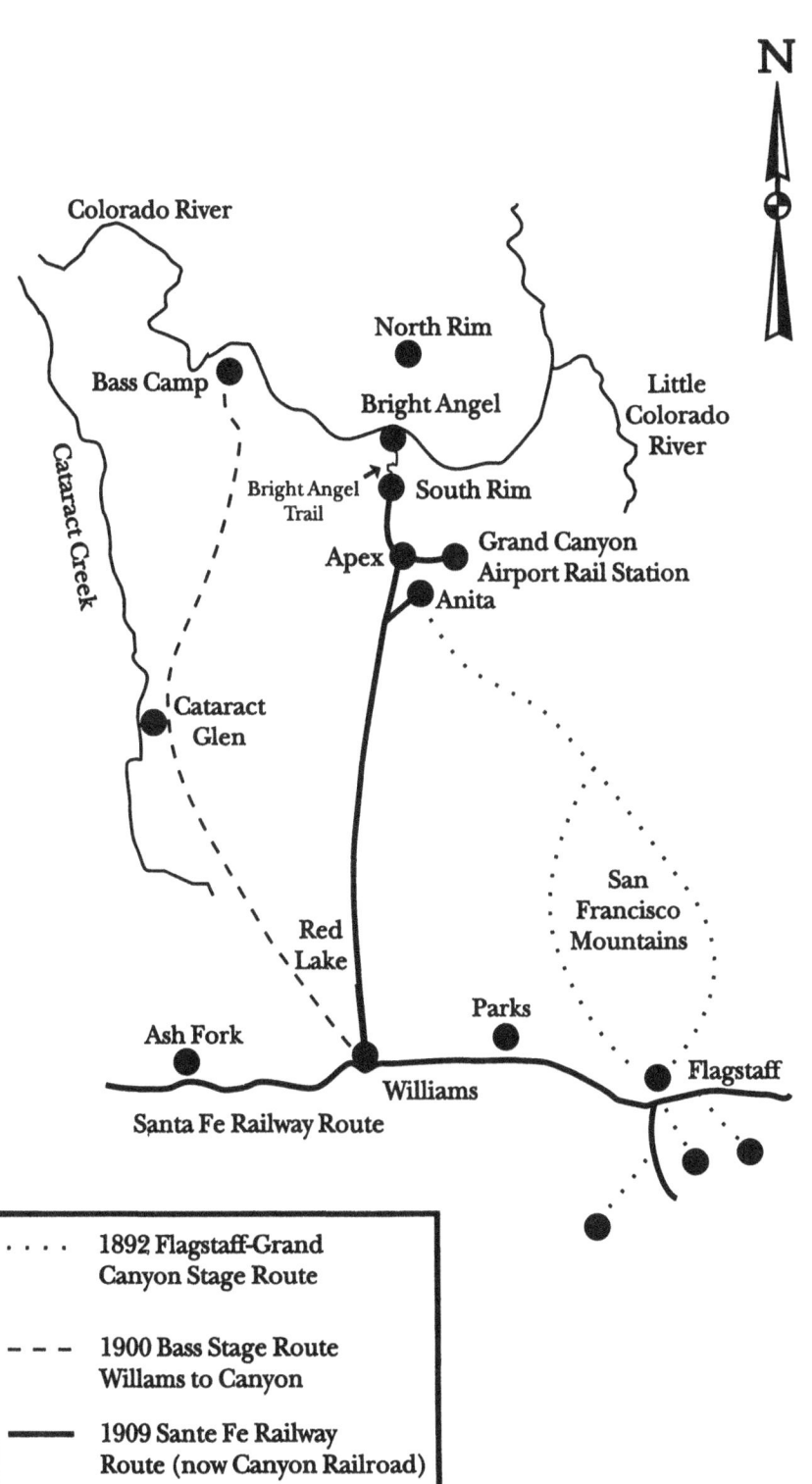

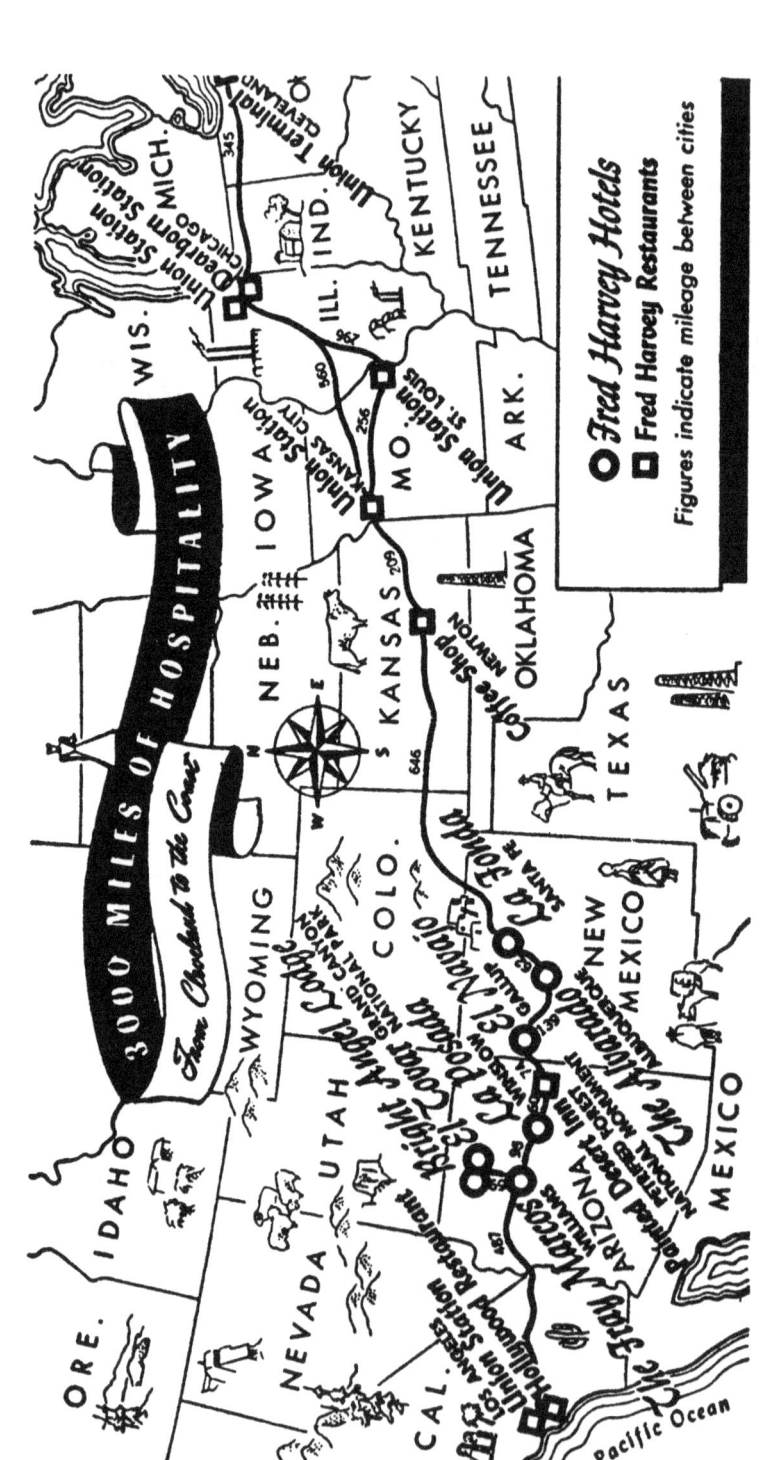

1
Distant Beginnings

IN 1869, CYRUS K. HOLLIDAY, the president of the Santa Fe Railway (then called the "Atlantic and Pacific"), was speaking enthusiastically of the future of his railroad, which at the time enjoyed only seven miles of track in Topeka, Kansas.

"Imagine, if you please, ladies and gentlemen, my right hand as Chicago, my left as St. Louis. Eventually the railroad we contemplate will reach these two cities and, crossing at Topeka, the intersection of my arms, will extend to Galveston, the City of Mexico, and San Francisco."

Maj. Tom Anderson, one listener in the small audience, laughed and muttered as he stalked out: "Oh, the damn old fool! Lord, Give us a rest!"

Holliday's dream surpassed even the dreamer. By the turn of the century, under the name Atlantic and Pacific, the Santa Fe Railway linked the northern, southern, and western coasts of the United States and extended to its border with Mexico. It became the main catalyst for western expansion and domestication. Holliday's dream prompted exploration, expeditions, surveys, and the eventual transcontinental steel ribbon all the way to the Pacific coast. His system included the smaller but no less challenging line to the Grand Canyon.

Today's tourists to the Canyon traverse lands hallowed by Spanish-American history, Indian cultures, and the travails of pioneer pathfinders. A lot of western history lies under foot en route. Well before the coming of the railroad, expeditions near the Canyon touched many places memorialized today in the Canyon Village on the south rim as well as along the railroad. A close bond unites these early pathfinders. The first explorers who blazed trails near the Canyon prepared the way for military cartographers. They in turn prepared the way for the transcontinental railroad, which spawned the stage routes that eventually generated the Canyon railroad and the historic village around its northern terminus. These legendary but little-known forerunners of the Canyon rails merit an initial review.

THE FIRST CANYON EXPEDITIONS

Early expeditions over the Coconino Plateau near the Canyon's south rim fall into two different classes: northward explorations from Mexico, such as those by Coronado and Garces before American nationhood; and much later, westward explorations by American military men mapping a westward passage from the Midwest to the Pacific.

Coronado

The first Europeans to see the Canyon were two dozen Spaniards who were members of Francisco Vasquez de Coronado's expedition in 1540, which travelled north from Mexico along the present Arizona-New Mexico border searching for the fabulous cities of Cibola. Rumors circulating in Spain and Mexico pictured seven majestic cities of gold sitting somewhere in what is now the southwestern United States.

Spain's Nuzo de Guzman, a rival of explorer Hernando Cortez, learned from an Indian guide in 1529 that these rich cities sat in the southwestern interior of New Spain. The viceroy of Mexico sent Franciscan Marcos de Niza north to investigate. He returned to Mexico with an encouraging report. The resulting search for Cibola prompted the greatest organized treasure hunt in the history of the Western hemisphere.

In the summer of 1540, eighty years before the pilgrims landed at Plymouth Rock, the viceroy sent an army of three hundred Spaniards and several hundred Indians north across the Rio Grande. Coronado was their leader. In the course of his journey into what is now Arizona, he sent a party under Don Pedro de Tovar to consult the Hopi Indians living near Tusayan north of the San Francisco Peaks, which the Hopi called "the place of snow at the very top." The Hopi reported a vast chasm north of the peaks "three to four leagues across," spreading long and golden in the sun. Tovar sent Don Lopez de Cardenas to investigate whether this chasm might be Cibola.

In late September 1540, Hopi guides led Cardenas on a twenty-day trek northwest via Tusayan on an old salt trail to the Canyon rim at a point near today's Desert View, twenty-five miles east of the present Grand Canyon Village. Coronado Butte near Moran Point memorializes the place. There they gasped at the Grand Canyon for the first time.

For three days they tried to descend into the yawning gorge. There was no way to do so. Castenada's *Narrative of the Coronado Expedition* describes the effort:

> After three days Captain Melgosa and one Juan Galeras and another companion, the three lightest and more agile men, made an attempt to go down. They returned about four o'clock in the afternoon, not having succeeded in reaching the bottom. They said they had been down about a third of the way and that the river seemed very large. Those who stayed above had guessed some huge rocks on the sides of the cliffs might be about as tall as a man, but those who went down swore that when they reached those rocks they were bigger than the great tower of Seville in Spain.

"Bigger than the great tower of Seville!" Such was the first and last Spanish response to the Canyon. Their enthusiasm to breach this barrier was no help in finding Cibola. Cardenas reported the Canyon to his superiors with the news that it contained no golden cities. Coronado continued across the southwestern plateau searching for one of the legendary cities named Quivera. His expedition eventually returned to Mexico City, the quest for Cibola's gold frustrated. Castaneda's *Narrative* concludes:

> It was God's pleasure that the discoveries should remain

for other peoples and that we who had gone there should content ourselves in saying that we were the first who discovered it and brought word of it.

Coronado's quest for Cibola did accomplish something: it gave Spain the claim to the vast regions that today comprise the American Southwest, including the Grand Canyon.

Today, almost five centuries later, thanks in good part to the railroad, the footprints of these conquistadors still linger on the rim. The Watchtower at Desert View commemorates their first vision of the Canyon. El Tovar Hotel adjoining the Canyon train depot memorializes their leader. The town of Tusayan, eight miles south of the rim, recalls the Hopi villagers who guided them to the Canyon. In a far humbler way, so also does the ghostly train station of Quivero, the name of one of the mythical cities of gold, sitting forlorn and pastoral at milepost 20 on the railroad, forty miles south of the Canyon. So, too, does the railroad station in Williams, named for Fray Marcos de Niza, the Franciscan priest who accompanied the Coronado expedition.

Garces

After the conquistadors, the next wave of explorers near the Canyon were Franciscan and Jesuit missionaries seeking to harvest souls rather than gold. The Jesuits came to the Southwest in 1691, notably in the person of Francisco Kino, whose statue adorns the Arizona capitol complex in Phoenix. The greatest of the Franciscan fathers was Francisco Tomas Garces, a tireless missionary doing extra duty as an explorer and cartographer.

In 1768, while serving at San Xavier del Bac near Tucson in what was then Mexico, Garces persuaded the commandant at Tubac to authorize an expedition to Indian settlements in southern California and northern Arizona. His brother Franciscans working with the Hopis one hundred miles southeast of the Canyon at the mission at Oraibi—the oldest continuously inhabited settlement in North America—had already named the peaks north of Flagstaff in honor of St. Francis as early as 1629. They wanted to be part of an established mission route like the one in Baja California.

Garces intended to develop a chain of missions linking Santa Fe and the California coast via old Indian routes through northern Arizona. In 1775, he set out with Juan Bautista de Anza to establish missions in the region termed Alta California. During this trek Anza founded the city of San Francisco. Garces then left his companions on the coast and travelled eastward into Arizona along his proposed mission trail toward Oraibi.

In the summer of 1776, as the American Revolution was erupting on the far side of the continent, Garces travelled alone through northern Arizona and touched the present sites of Peach Springs, Williams, and the south rim of the Canyon. His route roughly paralleled today's Canyon railroad. He passed north of the site of Williams, wound through Sitgreaves Mountain, and crossed Cataract Creek—*Rio Jabesua* (Havasupai Creek) he named it. He moved north with the San Francisco Peaks on his right and camped in Red Horse Wash, which today flows under the Canyon railroad. He reached the rim on June 26, 1776.

The Canyon struck him as it had Coronado: an impenetrable barrier. He wrote:

> I stopped in sight of the succession of deep gorges among which flows the river. From here I saw that in a very large mountain range extending from southeast to northwest and blue with distance a deep passage was cut, steep-sided like a man-made trough, through which the Colorado River ["Rio Colorado"] enters these lands; I called it the Puerto de Bucareli.

Garces was the first white man to see the Canyon from its west rim. During his five days of feasting with the Havasupai, then as now living in the Canyon's bottom, he gave the Colorado River its lasting name. "Colorado" has remained for the river. His name for the Canyon—*Puerto de Bucareli* (Bucareli Pass), given in honor of the viceroy of New Spain—has not remained. The place where he first viewed the Canyon is near Lipan Point.

In his notes, *barrier* is the recurring theme. Garces stands in awe at the immensity of that barrier. "I am astonished," he writes, "at the barrier which nature has fixed there." He concludes by describing the Canyon as "that calaboose [prison] of cliffs and canyons."

His story has a tragic but noble end. In 1781, blunders by Spanish officials inflamed the Yuma Indians, who turned against them. On his deathbed, Garces rebuked a fellow Spaniard who blamed them for the uprising. "Let us forget whose fault it is," he said, "and simply consider it God's punishment for our sins." The Havasupai Indians in the Canyon honor his name to this day.

AMERICAN EXPLORERS

Antoine Leroux

The first American native to explore the areas adjoining the Canyon was Antoine Leroux. A companion of Kit Carson and nearly as famous, he became an outstanding figure among mountain men roaming the West before the Civil War. Born and raised in St. Louis, he spoke English and French fluently and had a working knowledge of Spanish. In 1822, he moved west and settled near Taos, New Mexico, near the end of the Santa Fe Trail, where he made his living as a mountain man, guide, and scout. He blazed trails in the vast lands lying between Santa Fe and California, with much of his time spent in the Flagstaff-Williams area. He led four major expeditions across Arizona. Subsequent railroad surveys followed his routes, several with him as their guide.

Leroux died July 30, 1861, exhausted from his explorations. His body lies in the nave of the parish church in Taos where he worshipped, a token of the esteem he earned. His memory lives on near the Canyon. A major street in Flagstaff honors him, as does the finest spring in the San Francisco Peaks.

Bill Williams

While trapping on a northwestern Arizona stream in 1837, Leroux came upon Bill Williams, the famed trapper and mountain man, a character no less than Leroux. The two became friends; they had hunting, fishing, trailblazing, and roughhousing in common.

Born in 1787 in North Carolina, William Sherley Williams settled at an early age in St. Louis, even then the gateway to the West. There he learned about the Osage living in the Ozarks, to whom he became a Methodist missionary. While there he fell in love with an Osage maiden, who died a few years after bearing his two daughters.

His life among the Osage revealed major contradictions: he had gone to them to convert them to Christianity and the lifestyle of the whites; instead he became converted to their lifestyle and some of their beliefs. He became other things to other audiences: an itinerant preacher, scout, trailblazer, mountain man, and "Old Lone Wolf" to the Indians, who usually counted him a friend. As he moved west, his favorite travel areas became northern Arizona and southern Colorado.

In 1848, when the Lone Wolf was sixty-two years old, he set out to guide an expedition through southern Colorado. John Fremont, even then known as "Pathfinder," needed an expert to guide his group. Fremont, incidently, later became governor of the Arizona territory from 1878 to 1882, causing the naming of one of the San Francisco Peaks for him—an honor, like that of Pathfinder, which he poorly deserved. In the 1848 expedition, Williams argued against Fremont's bullheaded plan to go through a snowy pass and refused to lead the expedition as Fremont wished. Fremont then led the group into the pass himself and the group had to camp in snow caves where many froze to death. When the reputed Pathfinder escaped unscathed, he blathered to the West that the disaster was the fault of Bill Williams, whom he accused of poor guidance and desertion.

Old Bill's pride was hurt. With Fremont's medical officer, Benjamin Kern, he returned to the snowy pass for surveying instruments hidden in the snow. On March 14, 1848, he and Kern were killed by Ute Indians who stumbled across them by chance and failed to recognize either. Upon his death a western newspaper wrote:

> Thus died Bill Williams—a fair specimen of the old mountaineer—a set of men now nearly extinct; a set of men who possessed warm hearts, had noble purposes and as courageous spirits as could be found in any state or society:

Rude and unpolished but tender and true, firm in a fight but gentle as a woman to misfortune and distress—true Paladins of the mountains and plains.

According to Francis Inman's *The Old Santa Fe Trail,* Bill Williams knew every pass in the Rocky Mountains "better than any other man of his time." His ghost still inhabits one of them. Williams, Arizona, and its 9,256-ft. mountain to the south memorialize his name, along with the gushing stream called Bill Williams Fork.

Two years after Williams' death, Leroux suggested to the cartographers of the Sitgreaves expedition that they give the mountain his name, which it bears to this day. A rumor of many years vintage has it that Old Bill's ghost dwells atop his mountain. His true resting place is in southern Colorado, but a burial site on the top of his mountain probably would have pleased him. It certainly was to the liking of the early Santa Fe Railway. From 1901 to 1909, its advertisements repeatedly claimed that passengers changing from main line to Canyon trains in Williams, Arizona, could visit his grave atop his mountain. Today Old Bill is memorialized in the name Williams Flyer, given to one of the Grand Canyon trains.

MILITARY EXPEDITIONS

The southwest territory acquired from Spain in 1848 was almost totally uncharted. Honest maps of the period show large blank areas for what is now Arizona and New Mexico. Less honest maps of the day gratuitously show these areas richly dotted with deposits of gold and silver. To map and assess its true riches, including its potential for a railroad, Congress began sending military expeditions into the Southwest. One of the first of these was the Sitgreaves expedition.

Sitgreaves Expedition

In 1851, Congress commissioned Capt. Lorenzo Sitgreaves to move from New Mexico across the Colorado Plateau to the Colorado River to establish a western extension of the Santa Fe Trail. With Leroux as his guide, Sitgreaves and his party launched their expedition along the thirty-fifth parallel. Maj. H. L. Kendrick of the Second Artillery accompanied him as military escort. Sitgreaves' party numbered fifty, with twice as many mules.

He passed and named the Great Falls of the Little Colorado River. He wanted to proceed due west but Leroux warned him not to do so—if he continued west, Leroux warned, he would enter a "great canon," which had no exit. Sitgreaves' hope to reach the river inside the "great canon" proved impossible. He turned his party southwest toward the San Francisco Peaks, passed near the sites of Flagstaff and Williams and camped at Government Mountain west of Flagstaff. He reported back to Washington after his trek that his route was well suited for a western railroad.

Whipple Expedition

In 1853, Congress authorized another survey to determine the best travel route from the Midwest to the Pacific, with Lt. Amiel Weeks Whipple of Massachusetts as leader. In 1853-54, with Leroux paid $2,400 as guide, he moved from Fort Smith west along the thirty-fifth parallel through northern Arizona toward California. He passed close enough to the Canyon to name Red Butte, 20 miles to its south, and Leroux Wash and Leroux Spring near Flagstaff. With a hundred engineers, cartographers, geologists, and guides, Whipple's company camped in December 1853 near the San Francisco Peaks and noted the beauty of the surroundings:

> Following the course of the open, meadow-like valley, irrigated by the waters of Leroux's spring, we passed southeast and east about four miles and discovered a small stream flowing toward the great southern valley and forming probably the main branch of the Rio Verde.... From the San Francisco springs we passed over a spur from the hills and encamped near the southeast point of the mountains.

The next day they set out west of the peaks. The German naturalist Möllhausen, the first to sketch the Canyon, again records their admiration for the scenery:

> Four great peaks, covered with dazzling snow, rose high above the rest, and though numerous summits thronged

around and seemed connected with them—perhaps had grown out of them—that only tended to complete their unmistakeably volcanic character.

After camping near Laws Spring near milepost 15 on the present Canyon railroad, they then followed Sitgreaves' trail, made two years earlier, through Government Prairie. By January 6, they were back to the peaks again. Whipple had found a pass south of the San Francisco Peaks and south of Sitgreaves Mountain suitable for a rail line. The party then continued its explorations westward. After reaching the Colorado River, they turned north and crossed at Needles, which Whipple also named. In his final report to Washington, he wrote, "There is no doubt remaining that for construction of a railway the route we have passed over is . . . eminently advantageous."

Whipple later served as a topographical engineer in the Civil War. He was mortally wounded at the Battle of Chancellorsville in 1863. Prescott's Camp Whipple, later known as Fort Whipple, honors his memory. Early Santa Fe railroad maps show its westward routes coinciding with his trails.

Beale Expedition

Hearing the West's increasing demands for communication with the rest of the nation, Congress in 1857 authorized $50,000 under the Pacific Wagon Road Program to reconnoiter a railroad and, in the interim, to build a road for wagons and travellers moving from the Midwest to California. Secretary of War John B. Floyd selected Navy lieutenant Edward Fitzgerald Beale to blaze this trail.

Born in 1822 in Washington, D.C., a graduate of the Naval Academy, Beale had been with Kit Carson's men who joined Kearny's column in the Mexican border campaign. In 1848, he was the first to bring accurate news to Washington about the California gold discovery. He now had the task to survey and create a western wagon road almost a third of the way across the nation as a preliminary approximation for a railroad. He was also testing a curious theory of Jefferson Davis to see if camels could become as useful as horses as beasts of burden.

The army purchased camels in Asia Minor, hired Arabian

camel drivers, and shipped both to Texas. From there they joined Beale's party in New Mexico. In mid-1857, Beale lined up his men and camels (all "lovable and docile," as he called both of them) and plodded west along the thirty-fifth parallel. His caravan consisted of 22 camels, 8 wagons, 2 ambulances loaded with surveying equipment, and a herd of 350 sheep and 56 men, some in Arabian dress. By September 11, 1857, he was at the base of the San Francisco Peaks, which, he noted, "look down frowning on us." He travelled northwest over Spring Valley about 15 miles north of Williams. For a mile and a half there, his road coincides with the present Canyon rail line. His strange entourage of Arabs, ambulances, camels, and sheep camped at Laws Spring near milepost 15 on the railroad.

Returning to Washington in 1859, Beale wrote to Secretary Floyd:

> A year in the wilderness ended! During this time I have conducted my party from the Gulf of Mexico to the shores of the Pacific Ocean and back again to the eastern terminus of the road, through a country for the most part entirely unknown and inhabited by hostile Indians, without the loss of a man. I have tested the value of the camels, marked a new road to the Pacific, and travelled 4000 miles without an incident.

Beale concluded that his route was the most advantageous for a western railroad. "It is the shortest, the best timbered, the best grassed, the best watered," he wrote, adding that from the standpoint of its grade, it is "better than any other line between the two oceans with which I am acquainted."

Beale's final trip over his wagon road in 1859 solidifed the railroad explorations and surveys along the thirty-fifth parallel. Although his wagon road was only a dirt roadway cleared of boulders and trees, it became the country's great emigrant road from Santa Fe, New Mexico, to California from 1859 to 1882, when the rails arrived in Arizona and California. As early as 1884, the Santa Fe railroad issued route maps showing how its rails followed Beale's wagon road.

Beale lives on in the Canyon area. There is a Beale Point in the Canyon, a Beale's Spring in Mohave County, and a Beale

Mountain and a Beale Spring just east of the Canyon railroad about fourteen miles north of Williams. Remnants of his wagon road—now a proposed National Historic Trail—run adjacent to the Canyon railroad and cross it fifteen miles north of Williams. Inscriptions by his men dating from the 1857 trek still decorate boulders at his campsite at ms Spring near milepost 15 on the Canyon railroad.

In 1864, under the name "Atlantic and Pacific," the Santa Fe Railway received its congressional land grant. It celebrated by publishing its contemplated routes from the Midwest to the Pacific. On that map the Grand Canyon appears as a "Big Canon," on both sides of which are located unnamed "Indians."

Palmer

The engineer who finally fixed the rails along the thirty-fifth parallel route was William Jackson Palmer. Born in 1836, he had received the congressional Medal of Honor for bravery under fire in the Civil War. Congress sent him west to determine the best rail route. From the beginning, he favored the thirty-fifth parallel route through northern Arizona. He observed that the distance from Kansas City to San Francisco and to San Diego via the thirty-fifth parallel was hundreds of miles shorter than via the competing proposal along the thirty-second parallel. The thirty-fifth parallel offered better grades and freedom from hostile Indians, plus inexhaustible timber, ballast, and water. Beale had said much the same; Palmer now concurred with that judgment.

Palmer was especially enthusiastic about the route south of the Canyon:

> In crossing the Mogollon Range, we have the finest country met with, perhaps, on the entire route. It is the famous San Francisco Mountain Country, magnificently timbered, well watered, and covered winter and summer with the most nutritious grama grass. Its soil . . . will produce, without irrigation, wheat, barley, oats and potatoes in the heaviest crops. The summit and slopes of this range are dotted everywhere with beautiful little grassy parks, openings in the virgin forest of gigantic pines which cover the mountains.

In 1867, Palmer moved west over the Colorado Plateau south of the Canyon. He named Mount Agassiz in the San Francisco Peaks in honor of Jean Louis Rodolphe Agassiz, his Swiss-born zoologist companion, who made fossil studies of the area. His naturalist companion, Dr. C. C. Parry, a geologist, raved about the expected rail route because of its access to the great "canon" rumored to be nearby:

> The most attractive place of summer resort on the line of the road will be met with here on Mt. Agassiz [Flagstaff]. It has every attraction: health, scenery, sky, water, elevation, climate and proximity to the greatest natural curiosity known on this continent—the "Grand Canon" of the Colorado River, from which it is distant some 40 or 50 miles.

In 1869, Palmer concluded his report to Washington with a detailed map, the first to use the name "Grand Canyon." He recommended the thirty-fifth parallel route and suggested financial assistance to hasten the rails.

Along with those of Sitgreaves, Whipple, and Beale, Palmer's survey eventually generated two major rail lines: the east-west Atlantic and Pacific Railway of the 1880s and the later north-south Canyon route. These surveys also generated not only the railway but also Interstate 40 and its predecessor, Highway 66, the first transcontinental highway variously called the "Postal Highway," the "Ozark Trail," the "Will Rogers Route," the "Main Street of America," and, most popularly, the "Grand Canyon Route."

The railroad survey information came to Washington to the U.S. Corps of Topographical Engineers. Andrew Atkinson Humphreys, one of its officers, evaluated the data and located the eventual route. He decided in favor of the thirty-fifth parallel route through northern Arizona on a trail roughly following that of Beale. In the process he bequeathed his name to Humphreys Peak, the highest mountain in Arizona, looming 12,663 feet above Flagstaff.

In April 1880, Lewis Kingman, a division engineer for the Atlantic and Pacific, set the line for the track from Albuquerque to the Colorado River on into California. He started from Albuquerque with a party of twenty-one laborers and five wagons. To no one's surprise, he found that the best route followed the expeditions of Sitgreaves, Whipple, Palmer, and Beale.

The Atlantic and Pacific officially opened through-passenger service on October 21, 1883. On that date, a through train left Albuquerque bound for the Pacific coast. It carried two hundred passengers and sported a sleeping car and a mail car. Its stops included both Flagstaff and Williams, where some hardy souls disembarked to make their way to the "big canon" rumored nearby. The next year the railway published a system map showing how its trackage followed explorations of Beale, Palmer, and Whipple.

2

Stagecoaches to the Canyon

INTEREST IN GETTING to the Canyon developed simultaneously with the westward explorations of the cartographers and railroaders. Because the Atlantic and Pacific rails passed through northern Arizona, the early hamlets of Flagstaff and Williams became convenient departures for stagecoaches, as did Peach Springs, Maine, and Ash Fork. Stages became a harbinger of the future Canyon rails. They also shaped the development of the village on the rim.

Peach Springs

The Atlantic and Pacific's closest stop to the Canyon was at Peach Springs near what is today the Hualapai Indian Reservation. In the early 1880s, a few tourists tried to enter the Canyon from this stop by hiking down Peach Springs Wash via Lost Man Creek to Diamond Creek and then several miles along the creek to the river. In 1884, J. H. Farlee built a frame hotel near the junction of the creek and the river, twenty-three miles from Peach Springs. He then started a stage line from the railhead to his hotel.

The Farlee hotel was a true shanty: it had a single room and lean-to kitchen on the bottom floor and two small bedrooms above. It was the first hotel for the Canyon. His was also the Canyon's first stage. Neither had that honor for long. Primitive conditions coupled with the lack of a supporting town doomed both stage and hotel by 1889.

The Flagstaff Stages

With the Atlantic and Pacific's arrival in Flagstaff in 1882, passengers desiring to go onto the Canyon began to arrive in increasing numbers. In 1885, John ("Captain") Hance and William ("Bill") Hull began to cater to this trade as tour guides with makeshift farm wagons.

The more colorful of the two, Hance was born in Tennessee and had worked for a time in Kansas with "Tame Bill" Hickok, the brother of the more famous "Wild Bill" Hickok. A unique character from his youth, Hance claimed, probably with justification, to have fought on both sides in the Civil War.

Hance came to Arizona in 1868. When he first saw the Canyon in 1883, he found he could not leave it. He built a small cabin on the rim that he named Grandview, thirteen miles east of the present village. His was the first commercial establishment at the rim; it seemed at the time destined to become the core of the Canyon's tourist development.

In 1884, he staked out a tortuous, 5-hour-long trail now known as the Old Hance Trail leading down from his camp on the rim to his asbestos mine on the north bank of the river. He guided tourists into the Canyon for $12 a day, plus $1 per person for use of his trail. He set up tents at his homestead at the rim and made his cabin in Red Canyon his headquarters at the bottom.

In 1894, rockslides from a violent storm destroyed much of his trail. Rather than rebuild, he improved another Indian trail now called the New Hance Trail, which, although newer, was no easier: a narrow path zigzagging down the face of steep walls, over trees and boulders, across streams, at times disappearing in side canyons before arriving at the river rapids still named for him.

The Hance-Hull irregular stage service first picked up tourists on demand rather than on regular schedules. Hance's advertisement in the *Arizona Champion* of Flagstaff on September 18, 1886, resembles that of a pioneer travel agent:

Being thoroughly conversant with all the trails leading to the Grand Canyon of the Colorado, I am prepared to conduct parties thereto at any time. I have a fine spring of water near my house on the rim of the Canyon and can furnish accommodations for tourists and animals.

John Hance, Flagstaff, Az

Hance and Hull soon joined forces with the railroad to initiate a stage in May 1892 under the name Grand Canyon Stage Line. Replacing the Hance-Hull irregular farm wagons, the new stage operated on a regular triweekly schedule from Flagstaff to the south rim at Grandview, with shorter trips on demand to Walnut Canyon, the San Francisco Peaks, and the ice caves west of Flagstaff.

The stage covered the 80 miles from the Flagstaff depot to the rim in 11 hours in good weather. Summer stages left the depot at 7 A.M. on Mondays, Wednesdays, and Fridays. They returned at sunset the next day. The cost was $20 per person, later reduced to $15 to match competing stages. At relay stations en route, horses and drivers were changed. The second station at East Cedar Ranch, 35 miles north of the depot, offered rest and a 50-cent lunch. Crews again changed horses at Moqui Station, in the forest 30 miles south of Grandview. Accommodations at Hance's rim hotel cost $3 per night; dinner was usually an additional $1.

Hance found ample commercial motivation to ally his stage with the railway in order to bring passengers to his hotel, for en route on the stage he could bend their ears with reasons for taking his trail down to the river. Shortly after the stages began he arranged to accompany them as a guide. This role permitted him to regale captive passengers with glowing descriptions of his accommodations and his marvelous trail to the river.

Hance's hotel accommodations paralleled the luxury, or lack of it, of the stages. His hotel consisted of a central log cabin with surrounding tents. He assured his guests that they would not have to brave any fierce storms like that which had destroyed his trail in 1894, because his hotel was so solidly built. Little was said of his tents. His other cabin on the river was even more rustic, but it did offer repose to those who suffered down his trail. Today remains of that cabin still greet those who endure his trail to the river.

Among the first tourists Hance guided to the bottom were Mr. and Mrs. Edward Ayer. Ayer, a successful Flagstaff lumberman, and his wife eventually helped to establish Chicago's Field Museum and were major donors of Indian books to the Newberry Library there.

In 1885, Hance sold his stage to Wilbur Thurber, who also purchased the Hance hotel and toll-road trail. Hance then received permission to designate his headquarters at Grandview—the only available building—as the official post office for the Canyon. He called it "Tourist" and had himself appointed its first postmaster, an office he assumed in 1897 and exercised unti 1899.

In 1900, Grandview began to tremble at talk of a rail line whose proposed terminus would not be Grandview but some 13 miles west. Thurber began building a small tourist accommodation there called Bright Angel Hotel. Sensing change in the air, Hance sold out at Grandview and moved into this hotel. After El Tovar opened in 1905, the Fred Harvey Company hired him to entertain tourists with his tales of the Canyon.

One of Hance's favorite stories involved a rattlesnake with eight rattles and a whistle—the whistle, according to Hance, because the snake had worn out its tail shaking it at tourists. Another of his favorites was that the missing part of his index finger had been worn off by pointing out Canyon sights. And he also said that he himself had dug the Canyon during his mining excavations and had deposited the dirt at Flagstaff, where the mounds became the San Francisco Peaks.

With stories such as these, Hance became a frontier Aesop, offering up cowboy versions of Grimm's fairy tales to incredulous tourists. Among old-timers at the Canyon his name still recalls bizarre and incredible tales. His personality became the stuff of legends. His profanity was as spectacular as fireworks, and he was known as a terror when he was drunk—although, in his defense, these two traits were rarely exhibited around women and children and weakened in later life under the watchful eyes of the Harvey Company.

After its arrival at the rim in 1901, the Santa Fe Railway published a lengthy essay honoring Hance as seen through tourist eyes: "Captain John Hance: A Romantic Character of the Early Days of the Grand Canyon of Arizona." At the railway's invitation, Hamlin Garland wrote another essay about him for a railway promotional booklet compiled by its passenger agent, C. A. Higgins, entitled *The Grand Canyon of Arizona, Being a Book of Words from Many Pens* [1902, 1904, 1906]. Both essays portrayed Hance as a colorful frontier romantic almost as worthy of a visit as the Canyon itself.

Hance took ill in December 1918 and entered the Coconino County Hospital as an indigent; he died shortly thereafter. He now rests in the Canyon cemetery just west of the visitor center, close to the rim and the railroad depot where his funeral occurred. His headstone reads:

> Captain John Hance
> First Locator on the Grand Canyon
> Arizona Pioneer, Trail Builder and Guide
> Died Jany. 6th, 1919, aged 80 years

The Williams Stages

More serious but no less colorful than Hance, William ("Billy") Bass came from Indiana to Williams, Arizona, in 1883 at the age of thirty-four under a death sentence due to ill health. That sentence was stayed for nearly fifty years. He first lived in a cave near Williams. He soon found a job working on a cattle ranch along Cataract Creek. One day he rode his horse north with his cattle to Rain Tank Canyon. There, chasing some errant cows at full speed, he suddenly burst through the piñons directly onto the Canyon's awesome brink. "It nearly scared me to death," he later wrote.

Once at the Canyon, he found he could not leave it. Like Hance, he forgot about gold and found his destiny in the Canyon. For him, the gold lay in tourist pockets.

In 1885, he started a livery service in Williams. Three years after the railway's arrival there he launched a stage from Williams in direct competition with Hance's Flagstaff stage,

Bass's being the shorter by some twenty miles. His stages departed, as his advertisements put it, "according to the need and appearance of passengers." They left the Williams depot, proceeded northwest from town via Cataract Canyon to the Canyon, and from there to his "camp" on the west rim.

Rivalry between Bass and Hance was silent but intense. In the early 1890s, Bass built his Bass Hotel on the west rim, twenty-five miles west of the present Grand Canyon Village. His hotel was a small wooden structure rivalling Hance's accommodations far to the east. A 1901 guest there described it as "part tent, part wood, part rocks, part indoors, part outdoors." Like Hance, Bass gravitated toward mining. Like Hance, he built a trail into the Canyon's bottom to bring out ore. At the river, unlike Hance, he built and operated an awesome suspended ferry across the river—a steel cage swinging on a cable high above the water, large enough to carry horses, cattle, sheep, and human passengers over the raging torrents.

In 1892, Bass met an attractive tourist, Ada Diefendorf, a New York music teacher. Bass, who played the violin, and Ada, who taught it, married in 1894. Bass then sold his Williams livery to Sanford Rowe, no less a character, and kept the copper mine, hotel, and stage line for himself. He devoted his energies to improving tourist accommodations at his camp, where at times he and Ada would sit on the rim in the evenings and play music together to the hushed Canyon.

Initially, Bass stages from Williams paralleled the present Canyon railroad. Near the rim, at milepost 59, his stages coincided with the present rails. When the rails were being laid between 1898 and 1901, his coaches were in the best position to meet northbound trains. Bass stages met passengers at end-of-the-line stations—then called Anita, Coconino, and Bass—at mileposts 45, 57, and 59. From these points his stages transported passengers either to the Bright Angel Hotel at the rim or, preferably in his view, to his own camp twenty-five miles to the west.

The Ash Fork Route

In 1894, Bass moved the stage's southern terminus from Williams to Ash Fork, which generated a longer seventy-five-mile route requiring an overnight stop at the "Caves" midway across the plateau, where Bass had overnight and cooking facilities. The new route had tangible advantages. It was an all-weather course because of less snow. It allowed stages to meet Santa Fe main line trains coming north from Phoenix and east and west to and from California. Bass could entice eastbound passengers to his stages at Ash Fork before they reached competing stages at Flagstaff and Williams.

On April 15, 1895, Bass ran this ad in the weekly *Arizona Miner* in Prescott:

> Cataract route, formerly the Williams route. On May 1st and until further notice I will run regular stages between Ash Fork and the Grand Canyon of the Colorado River. Tourists are landed directly opposite Point Sublime at the head of Mystic Spring Trail, reaching the Cliff Dwellings, Grand Scenic Divide, Rains of Paradise, and Colorado River on horseback. No rope ladders or toboggan slides by this route. . . . I will run stages to suit the convenience of my patrons. Stage fare, round trip, $15. Parties of 10 or more, $12.50. Meals and beds, 75 cents each. For further information please address
>
> W. W. Bass, prop., Ash Fork, A.T.

The Ash Fork stage discontinued in 1901, when the rails reached the rim. Bass then began to use the rails as an adjunct to his camp. He established a rail siding five miles from the rim depot where train passengers bound for Bass Camp could disembark before reaching his competitors at the rim. In 1906, he built at this siding what his family called the "White House" and what village and railroad folk called the "house at Bass" or, simply, "Bass Station." The house and siding sat at the junction of forest road 328 and the rails, south of milepost 59 on the west side of the tracks on the road to Havasupai Hilltop and Bass Camp. A careful observer can still find traces there of the station's foundations and its one-car siding.

From 1906 to 1911, the Bass family moved back and forth from the camp to the White House during the tourist season. Despite these efforts, tourists did not flock to Bass camp; they preferred instead the growing facilities at the railroad's terminus.

Eventually Bass found his fortune in guiding tourists as they disembarked at the village depot. In 1911, he built another house less than a mile from the depot near the Canyon's first school, which he also built. Gradually over the years, his lengthy stage tours shrank to short trips from the train depot. On these trips he regularly recited his poetry to passengers and regaled them with his unusual, incorrect, and highly imaginative accounts of the Canyon's origins. Eventually he had six surreys and an automobile taking tourists on rim drives. In the exceptionally good year of 1915, he grossed more than $20,000, a large sum in those days.

Bass's intense competition with Hance gradually became redirected at the railroad and the Fred Harvey Company. The competition generated private detectives, fistfights, threats, and lawsuits. One by one, other tourist drivers were put out of business. Strong willed, fiercely loyal to the Canyon and his friends, stubborn to his competitors, Bass yielded an inch only to his allies. In later years, he became a respected but not universally liked figure.

Bass considered his long tenure on the rim as a mantle of authority. Toward the end of his stage days he published poetry and essays on the origins of the Canyon and the history of the village. He also wrote a semiautobiography of his love for the Canyon entitled *Adventures in the Canyon of the Colorado*, noting rightly that "my name can never be erased from the Canyon's history."

Bass remained Fred Harvey's sole competitor when the Canyon became a national park in 1919. In 1923, at the age of seventy-five, he sold his holdings to the Santa Fe Railway. At his death in 1933, his ashes were spread on Bass Tomb, a rocky Canyon promontory also called Holy Grail Temple. His wife, who survived him by eighteen years, rests at the Pioneer Cemetery west of the Visitor Center not far, ironically, from the grave of competitor John Hance.

The Williams-Parks Stage

In 1891, Fernando ("Ferd") Nellis started a third stage route to the Canyon via the small community of Parks, then called

Maine, twelve miles east of Williams. Maine stages left the Williams depot, travelled east to Maine, then north along the "Maine Road," now Spring Valley Road. This route, requiring ten hours in good weather, was shorter than the Ash Fork and Flagstaff routes. It passed through the majestic forests and meadows of Spring Valley, much praised by Sitgreaves, Whipple, Beale, and Palmer, crossed the vast prairies north of Valle, and then merged with the Flagstaff route near the Moqui Stage stop near Red Butte.

In 1892, Nellis sold this stage to Sanford Rowe, who had previously acquired the Bass livery in Williams, and now had the makings of his own stage route. Like Hance and Bass, Rowe needed a hotel for tourists. He heard in 1890 from Big Jim, a Havasupai Indian, about water near railroad milepost 61, three miles south of the rim. With Big Jim's help, he dug a well there and found enough water to support commercial facilities such as a log hotel, tavern, and entertainment buildings, which eventually became a recreation center for Canyon employees. Immediately south, he developed three mines still visible today, the chief one of which, Highland Mary, sports a residence visible at milepost 58 on the west side of the tracks. He developed his own stage stop and hotel two miles north of Highland Mary. For a time, this spot was the residence of the Canyon's chief ranger before the area became a national park. These attractions were torn down when the Grand Canyon became a national park in 1919.

Eventually Rowe sold his livery and stage to Martin Buggeln, a pioneer engineer on the Canyon railroad. In earlier occupations, Buggeln had been a deputy sheriff and cattleman. He added modern coaches to the Maine stage. He bought the original Hance hotel in 1906 at Grandview and sought to conquer the Flagstaff and Williams stage competition with his own two-story, seventeen-room hotel built at an area still charted as "Buggeln" on maps. His stage served this hotel, but the hotel was not successful—the center of tourist activity had moved thirteen miles west to the area around the railroad depot. Buggeln mainly used his hotel for family and friends until it closed in 1908.

STAGE TRAVEL

Stage travel was uncomfortable. The stages were top-heavy and poorly cushioned against omnipresent ruts and lava rocks. Often, there was no roadway. Snow and rain turned established ruts into muddy bogs. Horses and drivers seeking a new roadway were inevitably surprised by lurking volcanic rocks. Established routes became impassable during heavy summer rains in July and August and during deep snows in winter.

The trips varied in length from ten to fourteen hours, twice that when trouble developed. In case of accidents, drivers asked passengers to hold horses or make repairs or at least assist the drivers in doing so. The stages hardly kept the "hell for leather" pace suggested in romantic paintings of racing coaches and wide-nostrilled stallions. The ruts rarely permitted a faster pace than the ten hours on the Williams-Maine route.

This slow pace generated trivial pursuits. Drivers riding on top practiced markmanship by shooting rabbits, squirrels, and prairie dogs—a sport all the more challenging because the swaying coach made it more difficult. Some stages used a second or third coach attached as a trailer for baggage and provisions. Two or more horses were sometimes attached to the front hitch; occasionally they were harnassed to the trailer.

Horses undoubtedly suffered more than passengers. They had to face raw weather, lava rocks, ravines, and eat dust and mire as a regular diet. They were changed four times at relay stations, whose ruins can still be seen at Cedar Ranch Station and Hull Springs north of Flagstaff and at Moqui and Red Horse stations south of the rim. Some relay stations offered more than corrals: Cedar Station had buildings to house horses in bad weather, lodging for personnel, and a dining room for passengers.

Passenger Accounts of the Stages

Passenger reactions to the stage trips varied from wild enthusiasm to bitter complaint. C. A. Higgins, assistant Santa Fe passenger agent and a rider on the Flagstaff stage in 1893, was enthralled by the geography:

> The road crosses a flank of the splendid San Francisco

Peaks, descending to level stretches where prairie dogs abound, again winding through rocky defiles, on past volcanic vent-holes in whose subterreanean recesses the Cave Dwellers made their primitive home and where the hill slopes are thickly strewn with fragments of pottery; past bare mountains of black cinder striped with red slag; over broad ranges where sheep and cattle browse and the tents of the herders gleam from the hillside where the infrequent spring pours out its flow; threading the notches of slopes regularly set with cedar and piñon; across gentle divides from whose summits the faint rosy hues of the Painted Desert may be seen in the northeast, and in the north the black jagged lines of mountain ranges indefinitely far away; then once more into the pines and down a short, steep descent to the terminus in a romantic glen near John Hance's cabin.

In 1894, to promote its stages to the Canyon, the railroad published a detailed route map of the area between Flagstaff and the Canyon, which, among other oddities, showed a "Black Forest" midway between those towns and the Canyon in an area that then and now is only barren desert.

In 1893, Higgins assembled a rail travelog entitled *To California and Back*, which was later reissued as *To California over the Santa Fe Trail* (1907). The first edition assured prospective travellers that the Canyon stage was worth every discomfort, the multitude of which were unmentioned. Higgins later fitted his enthusiasm into the Santa Fe's subsequent, much-reprinted *Titan of Chasms: The Grand Canyon of Arizona* (1902, 1908, 1909, 1911).

Other stage passengers were less enthusiastic. Charles S. Gleed, an officer of the railway, took the stage just before inauguration of Canyon rail service. He termed it one of the "worst" stages that ever existed. "Many times," he wrote, "we lost our way and when night fell we had little hope of the canyon until the next day."

Artistic souls given to Victorian prose waxed more eloquent about the stages. Poet Harriet Monroe of Chicago took the stage in May 1899. Here is her flowery description of the route north from Flagstaff:

All the morning we had drifted through forests of tall pines and bare white aspens, watching the changing curves of San Francisco Peaks, whose lofty summits rose streaked with white against the blue, until at last as we rounded its foothills the desert lay below us like a sea, and we descended to the magic shore and took passage over the billows of silver and amethyst that foamed and waved beyond and afar.

She then describes the trip through the misnamed "Black Forest":

Our four horses kicked up the dust of the road and the wind swirled it into our faces and sifted it through our clothes. We had passed the halfway house where, finding the shanty too hot, we had unpacked and eaten our luncheon out in the sun and wind. It was just at the weary moment of the long, hot drive when the starting place seemed lost in the past and the goal far ahead. . . .

All day long we were alone with the world's immensity—no human face or voice breaking the waste of forest and plain, except when our tired horses thrice gave way to fresh ones, and their keepers came out from little shacks to unbuckle the harness and hear the news. After seventy-three miles, vistas of purple began to open through the trees, and the log cabin hotel welcomed us to our goal.

In 1899, G. K. Wood, one-time manager of the Flagstaff stage, published a booklet extolling the joys of the stage entitled *Personal Impressions of the Grand Canyon of the Colorado*. Here is how he described the stage trip:

The traveller is carried through some of the most beautiful and diversified scenery of the Rockies. The drive is sixty-five miles long, which is easily accomplished in ten hours, there being four relays of horses for the journey, so that the animals are always fresh, and the road being a solid mountain free from any obstruction, jars and jolts are almost unknown. The course is along what is perhaps the most beautiful scenery in Arizona or elsewhere. For the first twenty miles it lies through a beautiful forest of pine trees dotted here and there with parks, circling the base of the far-famed San Francisco mountains, past pre-historic cave dwellings and away out into the open prairie, relieved by tracts of scrub cedar and piñon trees, the home of the prairie dog and antelope. An excellent lunch can be procured at Cedar Ranch, thirty-four miles from Flagstaff, and thence once more away across the prairie through Cottonwood Canyon, where geologists can find much to interest them, one side of the canyon being about fifty feet wide, being composed of limestone formation while the opposite side is malapai. Then bounding over the prairie again until Moqui is reached, and a few miles further when the road again lies through the lordly Coconino Forest interspersed with sylvan glades and fragrant meadows for about twenty miles.

Such promotions offered more than a grain of truth about the magnificent scenery. They also promised a journey "you'll never forget," which, given the jolts and bruises, was as true as it was unmentioned.

First Stage Views of the Canyon

When the stage suddenly burst onto the Canyon rim, the trip became worth all its discomfort. Regardless of the misery, stage passengers uniformly expressed exultation upon seeing the Canyon. John Hance kept a visitors' log at his tent hotel where the inscriptions that are still readable there echo what one hears on the rim today: superlatives, sighs, and references to God's existence.

On July 9, 1892, stage passenger Mrs. John Z. Varme wrote in the log: "I have never witnessed anything like this. It scares me to even try to look down into it. My God, I am afraid the whole country will fall into this great hole in the ground."

Other comments in the log echo hers. "This is a warm place," wrote Gertrude B. Stevens on July 12, 1892. "I fainted when I saw this awful-looking canyon. I never wanted a drink so bad in my life." On June 5, 1895, Mary Hart, M.D., wrote: "There is a certain malady, commonly called 'big head,' with which a large number of otherwise healthy people are afflicted. Prescription: stand upon the brink of the Grand Canyon, gaze down and still further down, into its awful depths, and realize for the first time your own utter insignificance."

In 1892, the Santa Fe Railway gave artist Thomas Moran

(after whom Moran Point is named) free transportation to the rim in return for the copyright to his awesome painting *The Grand Chasm of the Colorado*. Moran arrived at the rim via stage. He describes his view in a letter to his wife:

> On reaching the brink the whole gorge for miles lay beneath and it was by far the most wonderfully grand and impressive scene that I have ever yet seen. . . . Above and across rose a wall 2,000 feet and below us a vast chasm 2,500 feet in perpendicular depth and a half-mile wide. . . . A suppressed sort of roar comes up constantly from the chasm but with that exception every thing impresses you with an awful stillness.

The Canyon was becoming for stage passengers what it would become for rail passengers: not only a tourist attraction but a Mecca offering the lure of approaching and even breaching the great barrier. As this lure became stronger, a railroad to the barrier became inevitable.

3

First Rails to the Rim

THE TRANSCONTINENTAL RAILROAD reached Flagstaff and Williams in 1882. First called the Atlantic and Pacific to suggest its cross-country scope, it became after reorganization in 1897 what it has been ever since: the Atcheson, Topeka, and Santa Fe, or Santa Fe for short.

The rails spreading across northern Arizona generated interest in easier access to the Canyon. Railroad plans for tracks to the Canyon's rim sprouted almost at the same time in several places and from several directions.

FROM WITHIN THE CANYON

Always quixotic, railroad speculation has never been more fanciful nor more fateful than the dream of Denver entrepreneur Frank Brown and his associate, Robert Brewster Stanton. In 1889, Brown organized the Denver Railway Company, with Stanton as its chief engineer. Stanton had engineered the famous Georgetown loop on the narrow gauge railroad west of Denver. The two planned a railroad to run from Denver via Grand Junction, Colorado, to follow the Colorado River, enter the Grand Canyon, and follow the river banks to the California border. Stanton promoted the thrill of this water level route as its chief selling point: it was a way to cross the Rockies, or a portion of them, without having to cross the mountains.

The first hurdle was to engineer this thrill, a task far more challenging than doing so on paper. Stanton studied Powell's diaries—possibly overlooking Powell's description of the Canyon's bottom as "our granite prison"—and concluded he had to navigate the entire Canyon by boat for the engineering survey.

The Brown expedition into the Colorado in 1889 was ill-prepared from the start. Their boats were lightweight, made of brittle red cedar, and lacking life preservers, which Brown had vetoed as unnecessary.

When Stanton first saw the boats, which Brown had ordered, he wrote: "As soon as I looked at them, my heart sank within me ... on account of their material—thin, light, light-red cedar." Loaded, the boats showed only four inches of gunwales above the waterline.

Several days after their entry into the churning torrents, violent rapids in Marble Canyon below Soap Creek Rapid hurled President Brown from his boat into a whirlpool. He surfaced twice and then disappeared into the heaving waves. He did not reappear. His crew was horrified. Stanton wrote of their despair:

> In the depth of the lonely canyon and beside the roaring waters, which leaped and lashed and foamed without ceasing, we sat for hours utterly paralyzed. We watched eddies whirl and then searched the banks for a mile and a half on either side in hopes of at least finding his body and giving it an honored burial place.

The body was never found. One of the senior crew, Peter Hansbrough, etched an inscription on the wall just below Soap Creek Rapid: "F. W. Brown, Pres. D. GC. & P. RR, was drowned July 10, 1889 opposite this point." The inscription is still there.

The worst was not over. Six days later, further downstream, another surging rapid catapulted two more crewmen from their boats. Both drowned. One of them was Hansbrough. Too dejected to etch another inscription, the survivors trudged out of the Canyon and returned to Denver.

Now president as well as chief engineer, Stanton did not give up his railroad dreams easily. In his view the very difficulty of river travel in the Canyon reinforced the need to replace it with rails. He also felt an obligation to his drowned companions to accomplish their original mission. In 1900, he returned to the Canyon with life preservers and stronger boats. He completed the engineering survey through the Canyon with one boat and much of his food lost, much gear washed away, and many injuries to his comrades but without further loss of life.

In his account of this trip, Stanton repeatedly reveals his railroad fantasies. One of the most romantic is his reflection on the spot where the Hance Trail meets the river:

> I dreamed one of my day dreams and saw each cove with its picturesque Swiss chalet and its happy mountain people with their herds of sheep and mountain goats, developing local business for our future railroad.

His diaries repeatedly describe railroad construction in the Canyon as easy. Where the Bass Trail meets the river, he sketched a major station named for geologist Clarence Dutton. He named the planned switchyard there the Clarence Dutton Depot Grounds. His plans were detailed; they included sidings, depot, buildings, and housing. Had his plans kept pace with his wild imagination, his rails here would likely have crossed under the precarious Bass cable ferry and mounted the side of the canyon toward the rim miles above. To his fertile imagination, putting rails up the Canyon walls would be no more difficult that putting them alongside the surging river. Nothing came of these dreams beyond his surging adreneline. Ultimately, for him as for so many others, the Canyon changed him much more than he changed it. Years later, at the request of the Santa Fe, Stanton wrote about his fateful survey through the Canyon in the railway's promotional book *Titan of Chasms: The Grand Canyon of Arizona*:

> I have often thought if the traveller on our great transcontinental railways but knew something of the arduous labors of those who prepared for him the luxury and comfort of modern travel, he might think with kindly feeling of the pioneers—the civil engineers—who made it possible to open up the wonders of our great western empire through and beyond the Rockies and who, in so many instances,

while blazing the way, laid down their very lives that he might travel in veritable palaces to and fro through the land.

Stanton undoubtedly was thinking of Brown and his fellow crewmen swept to their deaths on the first expedition. He continued with a hint of a lecture:

> Few travellers on the luxurious California Limited, as they branch off to take a look at the wonders of the Grand Canyon of Arizona, remember that some twelve years ago a railway was projected to run along the bottom of that deep gorge, and few know, perhaps, what it cost in hardships and in lives to make the reconnaissance and preliminary survey.

RAILS FROM FLAGSTAFF

Interest in a rail line from Flagstaff to the Canyon began even as stage routes were developing. Established stages were the obvious places to locate a roadbed. On December 31, 1886, the manager of the Ayer Lumber Company, D. M. Riordan, joined with other businessmen in Flagstaff to announce the "Flagstaff and Grand Canyon Railroad." On March 11, 1887, the territorial legislature exempted the proposed line from taxes for a period of six years. The *Arizona Champion* printed a rosy prediction of booming business: "Flagstaff has a great future before it and every one should help it forward and help those who are trying to help us."

On September 17, 1887, the *Champion* reported that forty miles of track were in place and that some traffic was moving on the line. On October 22, 1887, the paper reported that work had stopped because funds had dried up. In fact, no construction ever occurred; the progress reports probably had been circulated to drum up interest and investment.

Drumming up rail enthusiasm readily meant drumming up wild dreams. Rail rumors sprouted like flowers in northern Arizona. It was rumored that the Rock Island Railroad would build a line from San Francisco to the Colorado River, where it would connect with the Flagstaff-Canyon line. As early as 1892, *The Daily Star of Tucson* printed a story about "a force of thirteen teams" on the Flagstaff and Black Canyon railroad working from "Cliff Spur, fourteen miles northeast of Flagstaff." As the paper saw it, "the tourist and the scientist no longer would be deterred from visiting the wonder of wonders on account of the inconvenience of stage or hack travel." Soon, predicted the paper, tourists would be able to ride all the way to the Canyon "in a palace car."

On March 10, 1896, articles of incorporation were filed at the capital for the "Globe, Flagstaff, and Canyon Railroad," which was planned to run to Cameron Point on the Canyon's rim. Another "Grand Canyon Railroad Company" was incorporated in Prescott to run from Seligman to the Canyon, and yet another paper railroad was founded to run from Ash Fork.

Flagstaff was the most favored point of departure for these steel dreams. The Flagstaff *Sun Democrat* in September 1897 boasted that "it is only a question of a few months 'til a railroad will be built from Flagstaff to the Grand Canyon, and then the Skylight City will have a substantial growth and a rapid increase in wealth and population." As late as 1890, Riordan announced plans to extend rails north to Lee's Ferry and into Utah to connect with the Utah Central. He also partially implemented a north-south "Mineral Belt" to run from Flagstaff to Phoenix.

If all these plans had materialized, railroads would have entered Flagstaff from five directions: east and west via the Atlantic and Pacific, north and south via the Mineral Belt, and northwest via the Canyon railway. Not surprisingly, finances did not match these fantasies. The country-wide panic of 1893 curtailed them. Riordan went east to solicit financing and found himself unwelcome because financiers often disbelieved his story about a Canyon so fantastic.

Despite all the promotional braggadocio and setbacks, Ayers and Riordan's Flagstaff and Grand Canyon Railroad succeeded in surveying a route to the Canyon but did no formal construction. Other Canyon proposals did not reach the survey stage.

A railway from the Atlantic and Pacific main line northward to the rim made good sense. The impetus for doing so moved from Flagstaff to the smaller hamlet of Williams, thirty miles west. Mining rather than tourism became its catalyst.

RAILS FROM WILLIAMS

From the start, mining was the reason motivating the rails from Williams to the Canyon. In the process, mining and death again became partners. Miner Henry Ashurst, the pioneer homesteader and father of Sen. Henry Ashurst, died an agonizing death in the Canyon trapped beneath a boulder dislodged while prospecting. James Mooney fell to his death near the falls named for him while working a silver deposit. The Kolb brothers found a bleached skeleton of a nameless prospector in Granite Gorge. The story became somewhat the same in Williams, where miner Buckey O'Neill, the Canyon's chief rail promoter, also met an early death, although not directly from the workings of the rails.

The Canyon railroad story in Williams begins in 1882, when the Atlantic and Pacific arrived in that town. In 1887, when it relocated its division further west, it left behind in Williams an eating house, coal chute, stockyards, car repair facilities, employee cottages, a dormitory, telegraph office, freight house, and boxcar express room, all useful for supporting a branch line to the Canyon.

Into this rustic scene rode ruddy Irishman William O. ("Buckey") O'Neill, prospector, promotor, judge, mayor of Prescott, later to become one of Pres. Teddy Roosevelt's Rough Riders. At Tombstone and Prescott, before becoming "honorable," he had run a gauntlet of exciting western adverture s capturing robbers, swimming rivers, and pacifying the frontier. He had earned his name for his skill in "bucking the tiger" at the faro table. He had also read the inspiring account of the Canyon by William Randolph Hearst, the New York publisher who had written glowingly in the *The New York Journal* about his stage trip to the Canyon.

When O'Neill visited the Canyon for the first time, like Hance and Bass before him, he was so enthralled that he immediately built a log cabin on the rim twenty feet from its edge. Still there today, this cabin served him as a home-away-from-home, a base for prospecting, and a place for meditating on the Canyon.

O'Neill also learned something of the Canyon's economic potential for silver, copper, and asbestos. He filed a claim deep inside the Canyon at a place still known as O'Neill Butte and bought copper interests on the Coconino plateau twenty miles due south of the rim.

While O'Neill certainly liked the Canyon and his mines, he disliked travelling there by stage. He also needed a way to bring out his ore. Beginning in 1893, he began to try to convince Thomas R. Lombard, of the Chicago investment firm of Lombard, Goode and Company, to fund a railroad from Williams to the site of his cabin on the rim via, of course, his ore claims twenty miles south.

O'Neill preached the mining and railway gospel wherever he went. Williams residents caught his enthusiasm. In 1894, they helped finance a preliminary survey. O'Neill inspired enthusiasm by sending samples of ore to potential contributors. In September 1897, on the letterhead of the Office of Mayor of Prescott, he sent the following ore samples to the Santa Fe:

> Two samples of asbestos
> Sample of red ochre mineral paint
> Sample of yellow ochre mineral paint
> Sample of mica
> Samples of lead and silver ore
> Samples of gold-bearing rock—sulphurets
> Sample of copper ore

O'Neill bragged that all these samples came from the Canyon, where they could be mined in great quantities.

In 1897, thanks to his repeated invitations, Lombard and Goode accompanied him on a harrowing stage to the rim, with O'Neill at the reins. They were totally disenchanted with the stage, which reached the rim late at night. They had opposite reactions at dawn on seeing the Canyon. One of the investors was reported to be so overwhelmed by the sight that he promised O'Neill any amount of money if he could be left there forever to admire the view. The prospect's eye was apparently larger than his wallet.

Lombard and Goode were impressed by the prospects of big riches from the ore mines. Their own mining interests undoubtedly were more persuasive than O'Neill's or even the beauty of the Canyon.

Lombard

Lombard agreed with O'Neill's plan, got a map, and modestly decided that the railroad's northern terminus at O'Neill's cabin would be named Lombard to commemorate his magnanimity and that the mining area twenty miles south of the rim would be named Anita after his beloved daughter. The latter name has stuck. Had the former name endured, Grand Canyon Village today would be known as Lombard.

The next step was to get congressional approval for rails through the Grand Canyon Forest Preserve, as the Canyon area was then known. On May 18, 1898, the fifty-fifth Congress gave authority for the "Santa Fe and Grand Canyon Railroad Company" to build rails through the forest "by the most practicable route through a point at or near Lombard and the Bright Angel Trail to the Indian Gardens."

Canyon hikers know the audacity of this legislation. The railway authorized by Congress was to go not only to the rim (Lombard) but down *into* the Canyon, 4.5 miles of switchbacks to Indian Gardens—a route almost straight down. The unrealistic expectations of Congress about breaching the interior of the Canyon hardly differed from the fantasies of Brown, Stanton, and Riordan about the simplicity of building rails inside the Canyon, but the latter gentlemen had at least peered over the edge before announcing their destination.

O'Neill continued to press for construction funds. With George Young, the editor of *The Williams News*, he raised some $200,000, much of it from Williams residents, then numbering only 1,500 hardy souls. With cash in hand, Lombard, Goode and Company incorporated the "Santa Fe and Grand Canyon Railroad Company" July 31, 1897, with Goode as president—if Lombard could give his name to the terminus and his daughter's name to the mines, it was only fair that Goode should become president.

Building the Roadbed

On March 3, 1898, after a two-year squabble over routing, editor Young reported that grading was under way along a right-of-way due north from the east side of town. Roadbed construction began in June 1899; rails were first laid in October. The roadbed ran along a gently rolling country shaped like a bowl, with the highest points at the southern and northern ends. The southern end near Williams sat atop hundreds of feet of volcanic cinder covering buried limestone. About twenty miles north of Williams, as the cinders disappeared, the roadbed descended into a sloping depression worn smooth by winds, erosion, and the undulating motions of an ancient saltwater sea—the barren area that the 1884 Santa Fe Railway map had somehow named the Black Forest. The northern terminus at the rim became the highest point on the line because of the limestone uplift forming the Canyon's south rim.

Roadbed ballast came from volcanic cinder pits north of Williams. The line became a due-north course of sixty-four miles with spurs and stations at Pitt at milepost 6, Anita at milepost 44, Apex at milepost 52, and turnaround wyes at both ends of the line. The roadbed on the Anita spur sloped on a slight incline to permit ore cars to coast down to the junction without engine power.

Today, all these sidetracks have been removed with the exception of the wyes. Original roadbeds and sidings are still visible in many places. Many of the original ties remain in place, particularly on the 2.87-mile spur running to the mines at Anita, where ruins of mines, a makeshift smelter and tipple still sit in ruins under piñons and junipers growing in the old roadbed.

O'Neill did not live to see these exciting developments. After visiting his cabin, he sailed to Cuba with Roosevelt's Rough Riders to fight in the Spanish-American War. After preserving his life from the West's robbers, outlaws, and raging rivers, he lost it July 1, 1898, killed by sniper fire as he stood encouraging his front lines for battle. His death occurred the day before the famous charge up San Juan Hill by Roosevelt's Rough Riders.

Upon hearing of his death, *The Arizona Republican* thundered: "A Baptism of Fire," and heralded that "Captain William O. O'Neill was Sacrificed on Friday." The headlines continued:

> For the Capture of the Stronghold of San Juan. Arizona Mourns for him. A passage through the Valley of the

Shadow of Death. The Rough Riders of Arizona and New York were the First to Respond to a Call for Leaders to Open the Way.

O'Neill's name and fame are memorialized by O'Neill Butte in the Canyon, by his cabin still sitting west of Bright Angel Lodge, by his statue gracing the impressive Prescott courthouse, and by the Canyon railway's Buckey O'Neill Express.

Financial Problems

Despite recurring financial problems, rail construction moved onward in 1899 and into the next year. The rails reached Anita Junction at milepost 45 in early 1900. Intermittent passenger service began on March 15, 1900. The "Santa Fe and Grand Canyon R. R." issued timecards showing its schedule to Anita, where passengers transferred to the Bass stage for the remaining twenty miles. By June 1900, the line extended to milepost 53 in Coconino Canyon, and by October, reached milepost 55 deep within that canyon where passengers again transferred to a Bass stage for the remaining ten miles.

Construction problems increased in Coconino Canyon. One of the problems was the roadbed itself. Nowhere else on the Santa Fe system were there such abrupt curves and grade changes. Many of the curves reached the ten-degree maximum. These construction difficulties slowed progress. Furthermore, water shortages and a recession tarnished hopes of reaching the rim quickly. In late 1900, creditors demanded payment. The ore at Anita could not surface fast enough to meet their demands. The railroad's resolve weakened. Construction froze in July 1900, ten miles short of the rim. The company sold ore as fast as possible but could not pay its creditors, including its sponsors in Williams, who lost nearly all their investment. George Young himself lost $75,000.

In August the railroad went into receivership. A year later, at the federal courthouse in Prescott, it was sold for $150,000 to the Santa Fe Railway, which absorbed it and resumed construction under the name Grand Canyon Railway.

Arrival at the Rim

By September 11, 1901, the remaining track was completed through the Coconino Forest to the rim at a point near the present Bright Angel Lodge. The company then declared the line open for business. *The Williams News,* a prime supporter, was ecstatic. Under the banner "The Great Transaction's Done!" the *News* of September 14, 1901, announced the arrival of the rails:

> On last Saturday, as published in the *News* of last week the grade was completed to the rim; and on Wednesday of this week the laying of steel was finished. Considerable other work, such as ballasting and putting in the necessary "y" at the terminal yet remains to be done but as this is only of a secondary nature, compared with the great work just finished, it is scarcely worthy of mention.
>
> The first train to carry passengers from Williams directly to the hotel at the canyon will probably be run over the now completed road no later than next Tuesday, and with its arrival commences a new era in the tourist travel to this already famous resort for the sightseer. Thousands of people made the trip to the canyon by the long and tedious stage drive from Flagstaff before the railroad was ever thought of. Thousands more have made the trip since the completion of the railroad to the junction ten miles from the canyon; but now the entire distance can be covered by the tourist with all the modern conveniences of the railway of today.

On September 17, 1901, engineer Harry Schlee's locomotive 282 made the first trip with a load of 30 passengers and a bundle of mail in a baggage-coach car along with three water cars. The entire village of 22 residents met the train with cheers. The trip took three hours at the snail's pace of 20 miles per hour, but at $3.95 a ticket, the trip was a bargain by comparison with the day-long $20 stage trip.

The railway soon issued its first time cards showing a northbound train leaving Williams at 7 P.M., arriving at the rim at 10 P.M., and a southbound train leaving the rim at 9 P.M., arriving in Williams at 11:50 P.M.

The rails had arrived, and with them a birth of a new town at the rim: the Grand Canyon Village, and along with it a hint of civilization. The year after its arrival, Santa Fe passenger agent C. A. Higgins published a part-promotional, part-travelog, part-scientific book entitled *The Grand Canyon of Arizona, Being a Book of Many Words from Many Pens* [1902, 1904, 1906]. Available free at railroad stations and restaurants along the Santa Fe, the book played a major part in generating rail travel to the Canyon.

4

Civilizing the Frontier at Williams and the Canyon

THE CANYON RAILWAY PLAYED a major role in building the two towns of Williams and the Grand Canyon Village at each end of its line. Along with an Englishman, Fred Harvey, the railway made both towns receptive to tourists, more habitable for residents, and more refined for westward migrants.

Williams

In brochures issued after its arrival at the rim in 1901, Santa Fe promotions praised the hospitality and culture of Williams. In fact, turn-of-the-century Williams sported a life-style opposite most of these lofty promotions.

In 1882, the Prescott *Courier* noted that the mountains north of Williams harbored a large number of "professional robbers and murderers." It suggested that the military commander of the area place troops there to make those mountains "too hot for those fellows." Flagstaff harbored a similar dim view of its neighbor. In July 1885, the *Arizona Champion* printed:

> From the continued reports of the perpetration of crimes that come from Williams, we are led to think that our sister town is infested by some very lawless and desperate characters, as for nearly every week during the past months she has furnished some highly sensational occurrences; and her reputation for arrests and shooting affrays, for so small a place, will exceed that of any town in the territory.

The incident prompting this criticism was a drunk's murder of a relative of the justice of the peace. A lynching was averted, the paper adds, only because some "level-headed lover of justice filled the assassin full of buckshot." Such self-help was not at all out of step. "This, we think, was the most proper way to end the matter," decreed the paper, because such instant justice "saved the expense of violence and rope which would surely have been brought into use by the infuriated mob."

In 1881 the *Miner* published the following crime report:

Berry Brother's Store Robbed

> The store of Berry Brothers, near the Bill Williams' Mountain, on the line of the A & P RR, was robbed a few days since by three men who gained admittance in the night under the pretext of wanting to purchase goods. There were three men in the store at the time of the robbery, but they were covered by the guns of the highwaymen. They took what money there was in the house, 7 guns, 7 pistols, silk handkerchiefs, clothing, etc. When they departed they gave notice that they would return in 15 days. Two of the desperate characters are known in Colorado and New Mexico as King Fisher and Comstock.

On November 11, 1891, the *Miner* published another item about the railroad then under construction:

> News comes to the *Miner* from the line of the Atlantic and Pacific to the effect that on Tuesday night a desperate character made a fight, wounding two men, fortunately killing neither. The guilty party was arrested, and is now en route to the county jail. Shooting is all too frequent by odds on the Atlantic and Pacific line, and vigorous measures will have to be resorted to in order to check it. We never counsel violent or hasty action, but as the emergency presents itself, we say let there be a little wholesale hanging of bad characters.

Even the local *Williams News* was hard pressed to say much in praise of the hometown. In 1902, the *News* reported:

> There is a wine joint up at the western edge of town that should be suppressed. No liquor is sold stronger than wine. But that is the vilest "Dago Red" and would make a

man assassinate his mother. This joint has been the source of many brawls, especially among the Mexicans. Last Sunday evening two Mexicans, one armed with a pair of scissors and the other with a table fork, proceeded to make paper-box lids out of each other.

Another alarming situation on the Williams frontier was the operation of "hop houses." The town harbored a large number of Chinese railroad workers. By the turn of the century Williams sported twenty-three saloons and as many Chinese laundries, and according to some residents, in the back of each there was a "hop joint" for smoking marijuana and opium. In 1895, twelve Chinese were arrested and received fifty days in the county jail for smoking opium. The *Coconino Sun* complained that they remained in jail only four days and when they paid fines totalling only $150 they were released "to go their way and smoke hop again." In 1901, the Mohave *Miner* of Kingman repeated the claim that there are more "hop heads in the town of Williams than in any other town of its size in the United States."

In 1902, members of the Western Canada Press Association passed through Williams on the rails en route to the coast. One of the group wired this dispatch home:

> Williams is a unique town. It contains a population of about 1500 people whose principal occupation seems to be gambling. There are numerous fine saloons in Williams, in which games of all kinds, including roulette, faro, crap shooting, etc., are running constantly and more particularly on Sunday. There are said to be more shooting scrapes in Williams than in any other town of its size in America.

BUILDING EL TOVAR

Countering the rambunctious frontier were Edward P. Ripley, the president of the Santa Fe, and his friend, Fred Harvey. Both believed that the Southwest had great potential for tourism and western expansion, and each saw the railroad as the only western road able to realize that potential. Toward the end of the 1800s, they agreed to build a series of fine restaurants and hotels for passengers travelling on the Santa Fe. Described in the *Santa Fe Magazine* as a "luxurious spendthrift instead of an extreme caretaker," Ripley wanted the Santa Fe to have "the best line of station hotels in the world."

Some of the impetus for doing so came from needs at the Canyon. After the arrival of the first trains at the Canyon in 1901, the railway realized that a modern depot and hotel would be needed at the rim to accommodate increasing numbers of tourists. An original small frame depot sat just south of the present Bright Angel Lodge, on the north side of the tracks across from the wye. The small, two-story Bright Angel Hotel adjoined the site. To the depot's west sat Ralph Cameron's equally modest two-story, three-room hotel. In 1903, the railroad decided to build a huge, multi-story hotel of high standards about half a mile east.

Previously, the railroad had built its stations and hotels of functional stone or brick, often in board and batten style. The new hotel showed a major departure from these styles. The railway hired Albuquerque architect Charles F. Whittlesey to design it. The location selected was on the rim in a ponderosa forest about a ten-minute walk east of the original depot. The new hotel was first called the Bright Angel Tavern, after the Bright Angel Trail. The Santa Fe picked that name in hopes of appealing to hikers using the Bright Angel Trail, hoping to seduce them away from Cameron's lodgings at the top of that trail.

On October 1, 1904, the *Coconino Sun* reported that the name had been changed:

> The new Harvey Hotel on the brink of the Grand Canyon is nearly completed. As the work progresses it becomes more evident that for novelty of architecture and design and convenience for the tourist public, the new building will be unsurprassed.
>
> It has been decided to name the new hostelry El Tovar instead of Bright Angel Tavern. Pedro de Tovar is traditionally credited with being the first white man to penetrate into the mysterious depths of the Titan of Chasms.

El Tovar combined the qualities of a Swiss chalet, a Norway villa, and the castles of the Rhine. Its interiors sported a wide range of styles and accommodations, including an art and music room, a ladies lounge, a club room, solarium, grotto, and roof gardens, a library, and reading room. Furniture of oak and leather filled the rooms and public areas. Daily trains brought the best meat from the railroad's herds, as well as fresh produce. El Tovar's own herd provided milk and cheese, and a greenhouse ensured fresh flowers for rooms and tables. The Santa Fe's enthusiastic passenger agent, C. A. Higgins, contributed the poetic slogan carved over the first-floor doorway facing the rim: "Dreams of mountains as in their sleep they brood on things eternal."

El Tovar cost $250,000, a bargain for its day. Hopi Indians did much of the construction—appropriately so, since their forebears had led the Coronado expedition to the rim in 1540. The hotel opened with a flourish in January 1905. Soon, in folder racks from coast to coast, free for the taking, the railway offered two booklets to celebrate the opening—*El Tovar: A New Hotel at the Grand Canyon* [1905], richly illustrated with pictures of the gracious interiors; and *Hotel El Tovar* [1909], which showed the hotel as a solid building of rock and wood, with a circular entrance drive for horse-drawn coaches and a majestic view of the Canyon from the depot stairs.

The booklets lavished praise on El Tovar. The 1905 booklet, for example, went on in this vein:

> El Tovar is a long, low rambling edifice, built of native boulders and pine logs from far-off Oregon. The width north and south is three hundred and twenty-seven feet and from east to west two hundred and eighteen feet. . . . The hotel is from three to four stories high. It contains more than a hundred bedrooms . . . Ample accommodations are provided for 250 guests. . . . Outside are wide porches and roof gardens. . . . El Tovar is more than a hotel; it is a "village."

In the Santa Fe's 1915 *Grand Canyon Outings*, the railway again lauded the hotel as "the most unique resort hotel in the southwest," adding modestly that it was a "little village" entirely devoted to the entertainment of the traveller. It asserted that El Tovar was "one of the really unique hotels in America," possessing among its charms "all the comfort of a country club."

In addition to these booklets, the railway issued thousands of reprints of Thomas Moran's famous painting of the Canyon and sent them gratis to schools, offices, and railroad stations, hoping to inspire trips to El Tovar. Santa Fe passenger agent C. A. Higgins described the painting as "the soul of Michelangelo and of Beethoven."

These extravagant promotions worked: for many years business was so great at El Tovar that reservations were needed months in advance. (The same is still true.) Presidents Taft and Roosevelt were among its famous guests. So well known did the hotel become that some thought the Canyon detracted from its majesty. Naturalist John Burroughs wrote of meeting a woman at the hotel who complained that the Canyon was "built too close to the hotel." In 1920, writer and traveller John Van Dyke wrote that El Tovar was "too beguiling," because an indolent visitor peering at the view from inside would get the incorrect impression of seeing the whole Canyon.

A NEW CANYON DEPOT

The original Canyon depot, built by the Santa Fe hastily in 1901, sat immediately south of the present entrance to Bright Angel Lodge. That area, almost half a mile west of El Tovar, was the center of tourist activity when the railroad first arrived. The original Bright Angel Hotel was located there; it had opened just a year before the rails arrived in anticipation of serving rail tourists. Around the exterior of the hotel sat a cluster of tents or camps serving tourists who could not get other accommodations.

Just west of the hotel was the Cameron Hotel, a small, two-story structure that had been the former Red Horse Stage stop in the forest on the Flagstaff and Maine stage routes. Ralph Cameron had purchased the structure, dismantled it, brought it to the rim, and added a porch and a second story. He placed mining claims under the hotel, under the depot, and along the nearby Bright Angel Trail, which he operated at a toll of $1 for every animal, rider, and pedestrian.

The presence of the original depot in this commercial cluster suggested that this area would become the heart of tourist activity at the Canyon. Such was not to be the case.

After opening El Tovar, the railway decided it could foster El Tovar's fortunes by building a more spacious depot immediately south of the hotel at a spot well to the east of the commercial cluster surrounding the original depot. The new location had obvious commercial advantages for the railroad. Passengers disembarking from trains at this new station would gravitate toward the massive El Tovar looming above them rather than to the accommodations a half mile west.

Building a new station generated an outcry from Ralph Cameron. The new depot would take train passengers away from his hotel and his trail. He became a self-appointed spokesperson for the commercial entities adjoining the original depot. Thus began a long battle between Cameron and the Santa Fe and the park service.

CAMERON

Ralph Cameron and his brother, Niles, were early settlers at the Canyon. After arriving in 1883, like so many others of that decade, they went into the hotel and mining business. With Peter Berry, Cameron improved a century-old Havasupai sheep path into the Canyon, which, with typical modesty, he called the Cameron Trail—today's Bright Angel Trail. He controlled the trail but did not own it, although he treated it as his private road because he had the right to collect tolls on it. In 1902, the brothers acquired and re-constructed the Red Horse Stage station, named it the Cameron Hotel, and located it midway between the trail entrance and the original railroad depot— an ideal location for attracting both rail passengers and trail hikers. In 1904, they filed mining claims at the head of their trail, under the original depot site, along the trail, and at Indian Gardens, 4.5 miles down from the rim. They intended these claims to prevent intrusions into their tourist businesses, in which they had a large financial stake.

When the railway proposed to move its depot almost a half mile east, Cameron began a thirty-year dispute with the Santa Fe and the National Park Service, a dispute decorated with lawsuits and fistfights. He accused both of conspiring to squeeze him out of his hotel, trail, and mining business. For their part, the Santa Fe, the Harvey Company, and the park service differed from Cameron on how the rim should develop. These ideas did not include him, whom they viewed as a greedy businessman using mining claims to tie up spectacular public land for his own pocketbook. For his part, Cameron felt that as predecessor to the Santa Fe, Fred Harvey, and the park service, he had squatter's rights over these latecomers.

Notwithstanding Cameron's outcry, the railway proceeded with the new depot. It commissioned architect Francis Wilson to design a bungalow-style log station patterned after El Tovar. The two structures were to appear as a pair.

Built of ponderosa pine logs, not of Oregon pine like El Tovar, and costing some $16,500, the depot resembled a substantial log cabin, a sort of little brother to the massive El Tovar looming above it. It had station facilities downstairs and living quarters for station personnel upstairs. Whereas El Tovar had a frame construction with a sawn-log veneer, the depot sported whole logs and in this sense was the more authentic of the two.

Today, the station has a ticket area, dispatcher's window, waiting room, and outside carport for cars, buses, and trams. It remains the only log-cabin style station ever built by the Santa Fe; it is said to be the only log cabin railroad station in the world. The depot opened in the summer of 1910. It served the Santa Fe's passengers until the last Santa Fe train, July 30, 1968, and now serves the Grand Canyon Railway.

The opening of the new depot increased Cameron's ire at the railroad and park officials. He filed a blizzard of mining claims to retain control of Bright Angel Trail, which had been taken from him by Coconino County. In 1909, the courts held his mining claims invalid. Cameron still would not yield. At a press conference at the old Adams Hotel in Phoenix in 1912, he stated, "I have always said that I could make more money out of the Grand Canyon than any other man," adding, in view of the threat of losing his trail, that the Bright Angel Trail had been "only a side issue with me."

His continued toll collecting and control of Indian Gardens forced the railway and the park service to build separate non-toll trails into the Canyon, the first the Hermit Trail in 1911 at the end of the west rim drive, the second the more eastern Kaibab Trail in 1925. Neither was a toll trail; both were intended to put Cameron out of business.

Thwarted by the courts and his Canyon nemeses, Cameron ran for Congress in 1910. He was elected as a Republican delegate from the Arizona territory—the last territorial representative in Washington. In Washington he lobbied tirelessly for his personal financial interests at the Canyon. Where possible he tried to impede the interests of the Santa Fe Railway and the Fred Harvey Company. His leadership in the Republican party made tangling with him risky for those who had to placate politicans to stay in business. The railway, the Harvey Company, and the park service tried to negotiate with him but he rarely budged. He refused all efforts to cede his rights on the Cameron Trail to and from Indian Gardens, where he continued to press his mining claims and promote his tourist camp. No fewer than nineteen separate lawsuits sprang up over the first two decades of the 1900s. Eventually, in a 1920 decision, the U.S. Supreme Court hastened his departure by holding that the Canyon, as a subject of unusual scientific interest, is protected from private exploitation by the Antiquities Act of 1906.

In 1920, Cameron ascended to the U.S. Senate, where he continued to attack the National Park Service and lobbied intensely to replace the director of the park service. In 1922, he managed to have the Grand Canyon budget temporarily deleted from the park service. He secured passage of legislation giving control of Bright Angel Trail to Coconino County but retaining his right to collect tolls. In early 1924, he refused a chance to sell the trail to the park service. That same year was his undoing: on September 27, partrolling park rangers found eight gallons of mash stashed at his camp at Indian Gardens in a clandestine still near the entrance to one of his mines. Two weeks later the park service took control of his property there, confiscated his still, and urged him to leave. From Washington he launched an unsuccessful investigation of the Departments of Agriculture and Interior to try to regain his property.

Cameron had one last short-lived victory. In 1928, Coconino County and the park service sought to consummate an exchange of Bright Angel Trail for a payment of $100,000 in order to improve the former stage route from Maine to the rim, now known as Spring Valley Road. Cameron and his Washington backers defeated this plan for road improvements. His triumph was short-lived: in the senatorial election later that year, he was defeated and silenced by Carl Hayden.

THE FRAY MARCOS DEPOT

Shortly after completing the design for the new Canyon depot the railway commissioned architect Francis Wilson to design another new station in Williams at the south end of the line to match the depot at the north end. Construction began in 1907. The depot adjoined a companion hotel just as at the Canyon. Both structures in Williams were named Fray Marcos in honor of the Franciscan priest who had accompanied the Coronado expedition on the first European discovery of the Canyon. Now to the delight of the Santa Fe, both ends of its Canyon line memorialized the Coronado expedition in the same Spanish language as the railroad's own name.

The Fray Marcos replaced several rickety boxcars 200 yards east, which had been used for ticket sales, shelter, and snacking. Originally the hotel had 22 rooms for guests and 10 for staff on the second floor. Room 5, a two-room suite with its own bath, overlooked the tracks. Rooms 7-8 and 13-14 had a shared bath; all other rooms had a community bath.

Increased train travel soon required expansion. In 1925, a two-story addition of 21 rooms grew onto the north side. Twenty of the rooms were in adjoining pairs, each with its own bath. The two-room suite with fireplace on the northwest corner of the addition was for the manager. In its heyday, the hotel employed 40-50 persons, who received a monthly payroll of about $2,000, a considerable sum in those days.

The exterior of the Fray Marcos then and now defies description. Depending on the biases and architectural school of the viewer, it could be described as Greek Revival, Classic Revival, beaux arts classic, or simply as "Arizona concrete." In its brochures, the railway described it as " an old Spanish mission." Its interior was said to sport "a large Indian room," which the railroad claimed was "tastefully furnished in arts and crafts style." Whatever it is called, its unusual style merited its inclusion in the National Register of Historic Places, an honor now possessed by the depots at both ends of the Canyon line.

The hotel and depot opened for business on March 10, 1908. It boasted being the largest existing reinforced concrete building in Arizona. It probably still is so today. Both its architectue and its building material seem out of place for a structure said to exhibit both Spanish and Indian decor. The railway turned its management over to the Fred Harvey Company shortly after its opening, and from that date on, "Harvey Girls" staffed the hotel and dining room in the west end of the building.

FRED HARVEY AND THE HARVEY COMPANY

El Tovar at the north end of the line and the Fray Marcos at its south end were linked to the Canyon and the railway not only by the steel rails but also by the person and company of Fred Harvey. His story is as much a Horatio Alger saga as that of the railroad. He came to the United States from his native England with what amounted to ten dollars in his pocket in the mid-1880s. He washed dishes for two dollars a day in New York, saved his money, and started a small restaurant in St. Louis. There he eventually got a job in a railway express car sorting pony express mail headed for the West.

Harvey soon rose to the position of freight agent, a job requiring much western travel. As he travelled in the West, he noted the squalid eating facilities for passengers, who typically suffered twenty-minute meal stops in dingy track-side mess halls. Restaurants often were lacking in refrigeration. Food suffered from inadequate or unusual preservation. Breakfast, for example, often consisted of rancid bacon, canned beans, or three kinds of eggs—"ranch eggs" from local farms; "eastern" eggs from eastern dairies, where the eggs were preserved in lime; or "yard" eggs, which had been laid near the train depot.

The resulting railroad culture aptly described the meals and the service: the soda biscuits served with eggs were known as "sinkers" for their hardness. Diners could choose either cold tea or bitter black coffee called "engine oil." Waiters became known as "hash slingers," for the most frequent entrée and the method of serving it.

Waiters often served meals in the last few seconds of the twenty-minute train stop just as the train whistled for its departure. Frustrated passengers would rush back to the train and leave their uneaten food on the plates. Hash slingers routinely gathered up this food and re-served it to incoming passengers, ate it themselves, or took it home for their families, often splitting profits among themselves.

Harvey thought he could do better. For its part, acutely aware of its culinary shortcomings, the Santa Fe Railway needed inspiration for improved food service. The two needs complemented each other. Harvey began by buying a lunchroom in Topeka, Kansas, which he transformed into his first Harvey House in 1876. This restaurant was the start of his long association with the Santa Fe. Formalized in a first contract in 1878, their agreement gave Harvey operation of all Santa Fe hotels and restaurants along its vast system. In effect, Harvey became the Santa Fe's hotelier. Before the end of the century he had established Harvey Houses along the Santa Fe from Kansas City and St. Louis all the way to the California coast. In Arizona his elegant restaurants adjoined depots in Winslow, Williams, Ash Fork, Seligman, and Kingman as well as at the Canyon. His network included more than forty hotels by the time of his death.

The seemingly small asset of the Topeka lunchroom, coupled with the railroad's encouragement, soon made the Santa Fe one of the most luxurious railroads in the world. In the process, Harvey and the Santa Fe revolutionized train eating standards and lent an ambiance of refinement to the frontier. The relationship also spawned some humor about Harvey's thrifty ways: Capt. John Hance liked to tell train passengers at the Canyon that the Grand Canyon had been dug when Fred Harvey was scratching around on the ground for a dropped nickel.

The most elegant of Harvey's restaurants, like the El Tovar and the Fray Marcos, employed waitresses called Harvey Girls. They were usually unmarried local girls in their twenties who promised to adhere to Harvey's high requirements of discipline. More than 100,000 Harvey Girls worked for the company between 1883 and the late 1950s. Harvey recruited most of them through ads in the newspapers east of the Mississippi. Most who responded did so for economic reasons, although the lore of the West and personal romance were additional considerations. In the 1880s, their starting salary was $17.50 a week, plus tips, room and board, and paid vacations home. They lived in dorms where they were supervised by matrons. They were forbidden to marry for at least a year and had to follow strict conventlike rules. Despite the rules and chaperones, thousands of the girls married ranchers, miners, merchants, cowboys, and railroad men, and many of them named their firstborn sons after Fred Harvey. As Will Rogers put it, Harvey kept the West "in food and wives."

Harvey insisted on high standards in his eating establishments. Passengers needed to eat and be back on the train in twenty minutes. Harvey cooks and waitresses worked out a precise system to expedite food service. Incoming trains, such as those arriving at the Fray Marcos in Williams, would take a tally of passengers while the train was fifty miles from the station. The conductor then telegraphed the tally to the restaurant so that cooks and waitresses knew the exact number of meals needed. As the train pulled into the station, a Harvey Girl would bang a gong to signal waitresses to begin dishing out the food. A "drink girl" would come to tables and inquire of customers which they preferrred—coffee, milk, or tea. She would then position cups accordingly: up for coffee, down for milk, and on the side for tea. There were variations on this clue: a handle pointing to six o'clock meant coffee, pointing to three o'clock meant tea, and a removed cup meant milk. Whatever the format, the waitresses serving drinks could tell without asking what drink to pour, to the marvel of the diners.

Harvey held out a strict atmosphere for his diners as well: there was to be no profanity and no insults to his "girls." Men were expected to wear coats; if a diner lacked one, a waiter would loan him one. Flirting between passengers and waitresses was prohibited, although unsuccessfully, for many Harvey Girls met their future husbands while serving them their meals.

Harvey's food was intended to be first class to rival the best in the finest hotels of the cultured East. His beef was especially renowned. The railway arranged for its slaughter and transport via its own refrigerated cars. Harvey served specialty items at flagship hotels like El Tovar: Coney Island Clam Chowder, Long Island Duck, and Gulf of Mexico Sea Turtle—appellations geographically out of place, to be sure, but intended to suggest that the frontier could provide food comparable to the finest resorts elsewhere.

Waitressing at the turn of the century on the frontier was hardly a respectable occupation, particularly in such frontier haunts as Williams and the Canyon. Womanhood itself was suspect in the West: the popular saying was that there were no ladies west of Dodge City and no women at all west of Albuquerque. Harvey helped to change this image with high standards in the selection and work habits of his girls. He had a rabid aversion to dirt and disorder and was much impressed with military discipline. Under his regime, being a Harvey Girl meant having high credentials, manners, and organizational ability.

Harvey did not allow his girls to chew gum, to live outside the dorm he provided, or to wear any makeup, jewelry, or outfits on the job other than the back-and-white uniforms that became the Harvey Girl trademark. The girls had to be between 18 and 30 years of age, of good character, and willing to abide by the strict rising and bedtime hours. Being a Harvey Girl at the turn of the century was like becoming an old German nun, all starched and firm and disciplined.

Stories and legends grew up around the Harvey Girls. One involved Williams, Arizona. According to the story, a local prostitute there named Queenie Le Grand found her work falling off because of the arrival of the younger and more refined Harvey Girls. Under a fictitious name Queenie went to the Fray Marcos to seek a job and found Fred Harvey himself doing the interview. Harvey could not turn her down; he reportedly said to her: "I cannot in conscience turn you away from a job here at the risk of your becoming like that infamous Queenie Le Grand, that fallen woman."

Harvey employment offered Harvey Girls both a sisterhood and a safe haven in a rough land, along with an opportunity to forge a new life away from the homestead. Independence, self-esteem, travel to strange places, and the opportunity to meet interesting people added to the attractions of the job. Although some felt the job was slave labor, most enjoyed working for Harvey, especially at the Canyon.

In 1944, MGM produced *The Harvey Girls,* starring Judy Garland. The movie described the true life of a typical Harvey Girl along the Santa Fe. Advertisements lauded the movie as a "fast-moving epic," a "battle between the civilizing influences of the Santa Fe railroad and the Harvey House, as opposed to the lawless rule of outlaws, gamblers and crooked officials of the early West."

In encouraging tourist travel to the West, Harvey and the Santa Fe promoted the Spanish heritage of the Southwest and the Canyon lands. They designed and operated several major hotels with Spanish decor and names: the Alvarado in Albuquerque, named for Captain Hernando de Alvarado; the Castenada in Las Vegas; and the Cardenas in Trinidad, Colorado, named for Don Garcia Lopez de Cardenas. The El Tovar and the Fray Marcos hotels at the ends of the Canyon line fit eloquently into this tradition of conquistador-style service.

El Tovar became the crown jewel in this empire. For the Harvey Girls it was the most desired assignment. The scenery was the best, the clientele the most appreciative, and—not least of all—the tips were reputed to be the most generous in the entire Santa Fe system. Harvey Girls at the Canyon regularly could double their salary with tips.

Although Fred Harvey was aware of the Canyon railroad and the plans for El Tovar, he did not live to see the fruition of these dreams. He died in 1901. His last words were reputed to have been, "Don't cut the ham too thin." At his death his company's empire included forty-five hotels and eating houses along the Santa Fe from Chicago to the coast, plus thirty dining cars on the transcontinental streamliners. Other railroads could compete with the Santa Fe for luxury and speed but none could boast "meals by Fred Harvey."

After his death, some said of Harvey that he had made the desert blossom with beefsteak and pretty girls. He also left behind something more intangible: a touch of refinement for frontier outposts such as Williams and the Canyon. His company's high standards refined frontier habits throughout the West, notably at El Tovar. His presence is still felt at the Canyon: even today visitors sometimes turn up at the Harvey Company offices asking to meet him.

5

Travel Promotions

SHORTLY AFTER REACHING the Canyon in 1901, the Santa Fe began to publish extravagant tourist-oriented promotions to attract visitors to the rim via its rails. Promotional material capitalized not only on the Canyon and its majesty but also on the central fact that the Santa Fe was the only railway able to get there. Its advertising department determined to associate its name with the indigenous peoples and terrain of the Southwest to make a patriotic appeal to the travelling public to learn firsthand the unusual wonders of a land then largely unknown.

WILLIAMS AS THE GATEWAY

After its arrival at the rim in 1901, the Santa Fe announced that the town of Williams, where the Canyon train connection was made, sported "sawmills, smelters, numerous well-stocked stores and railroad division buildings. The Grand Canyon Hotel—a large brick edifice of forty rooms, with electric lights and first-class dining room—affords good accommodation."

Such was the railroad's advertising. The reality at times was different. The division headquarters moved to Seligman shortly after publication of this brochure. While the sawmill industry did flourish in Williams for a time at the turn of the century, ore smelters never did. With the opening of the Fray Marcos Hotel at the depot, the Santa Fe dropped mention of the competing Grand Canyon Hotel. In describing the "easy climb" of the 9,264-ft. Bill Williams Mountain south of town, railway brochures from 1901 to 1909 took major liberties with history:

> On the summit [of Bill Williams Mountain] is buried the pioneer scout Bill Williams [also the name of a famous Santa Fe train]. From his resting place there is a wide lookout on the eastern horizon.

This imaginative claim about Bill Williams' grave reappeared in the railroad's masterful, book-length 1908 and 1909 travelog entitled *To California via the Santa Fe Trail.* Although old Bill Williams, then as now, rests in Colorado, it was only a small matter to the Santa Fe. Its brochures and books repeatedly assured its public that from his resting place atop Williams Mountain, "Kendrick and Sitgreaves Mountains are also visible." While the view is accurate, the railroad neglected to mention that the turn-of-the-century ascent to the summit for this sweeping view was hardly easy, that there was a day required for the trip, and that a toll was charged those who tried it.

The railway was especially proud of its volcanic cinder roadbed to the Canyon. From the start, its advertisements described these cinders as evidence of the smoothness of its line:

> The railroad track to the Canyon is remarkably smooth for a new line. It is built across a slightly rolling mesa, in places thickly wooded, in others open. The snow-covered San Francisco Peaks are on the eastern horizon. Kendricks, Sitgreaves and Williams Mountains are also visible. Red Butte, thirty miles distant, is a prominent local landmark. The route here is amid fragrant pines, over low hills and along occasional gulches and "washes." Taken under the favorable conditions which generally prevail at this high altitude, the journey is a novelty and delight.

In fact, however, this "remarkably smooth" roadbed was unstable. It needed to be re-ballasted almost in its entirety because of the poor quality of the original construction. Between 1907 and 1909, the railway replaced the "dirt track," which was made of light rails that original crews had laid directly on the ground with heavier steel and put the roadbed back on much deeper cinder ballast. Chinese laborers mined these cinders from the huge pit still visible at Pitt at milepost 6, digging and loading them by hand.

PROMOTIONS AND SCHEDULES

Early railroad promotional material, such as the freely distributed booklet, *Titan of Chasms,* lauded the ease with which a rail passenger could reach the Canyon. The initial schedule of March 1900 showed trains averaging 15 MPH from Williams to Anita; later schedules were a tad faster.

Once El Tovar opened, tourists came to the Canyon in great numbers. The railroad added another daily round trip from Williams, No. 14 northbound and No. 15 southbound, for a total of two daily round trips, a schedule that continued until 1932. Along with its annual timetables, the railroad published an aggressive barrage of promotional booklets to encourage travel to the Canyon, including *The Grand Canyon of Arizona* [1912], *Grand Canyon Outings* [1915], and *Grand Canyon of Arizona: Santa Fe Pullmans to the Rim* [1936, 1937].

These publications featured glowing descriptions of the Canyon, accommodations at El Tovar, and the luxury of the train trip. Their appeal of a comfortable way to confront a seemingly uncomfortable land generated great interest and undoubtedly helped ticket sales. The ads emphasized the awe of the Southwest, respect for the Native Americans and their humble but unusual habitats. The unstated but recurring motif of the ads, brochures, and books was the suggestion that a rail trip west on the Santa Fe, especially to the Canyon, would awaken in any patriotic American a sense of nationhood.

ART VIA RAIL

Shortly after the arrival at the rim, Santa Fe president Edward Ripley encouraged its advertising manager, W. F. White, to expand the southwestern theme being used in its advertising. White hit upon the idea of using the Canyon rails plus free room and board as a means to entice famous painters to come to the Canyon, paint its majesty, and donate some of the paintings to the railroad. White got this idea from viewing Thomas Moran's famous painting of the Canyon, *The Grand Chasm of the Colorado,* which Moran had painted on his first visit in 1873. The railroad bought the rights to this painting and had reprints of it sent by the thousands around the country. Eventually it was bought by the United States Congress for $10,000 and hung in the nation's capitol.

Shortly after the rails reached Flagstaff, the railroad invited Moran to travel back to the rim via the new rails to paint other scenes for use in Santa Fe advertising. Moran's first visit to the Canyon had been via an uncomfortable horse. His second trip in 1892 via the Flagstaff stage left him again standing at the rim "astonished at the majestic spectacle," which he termed the "most awfully grand and impressive scene that I have ever yet seen."

In 1900, Ripley promoted William Haskell Simpson as general advertising manager. Simpson soon expanded on the Moran example: he sent other great western artists on three-to-four week rail excursions to the rim to capture its grandeur on canvas. Their trips were financed by an agreement to permit the railroad to have its choice of one of the paintings produced there. Those who came to the rim under the patronage of the railroad were the Who's Who of western artists of the day: Bertha Dressler, Frank Paul Sauerwein, Louis Akin, Charles Craig, Elliot Daingerfield, Edward Potthast, Carol Borg, and Warren Rollins.

The artists appeared to have loved the opportunity. Borg regularly was given room and board at El Tovar in exchange for a painting. Rollins spent so much time at the rim that the railway provided him with a studio near the train station so he could interpret the Canyon for railway travel posters. In 1906, the "Sagebrush Rembrandt," William R. Leigh, persuaded Simpson to provide him with a rail trip to the rim in return for a painting. His style so suited Simpson that the railway purchased five paintings to hang in the two lodges then at the rim. Gunnar Widforss spent most of the later part of his life at the Canyon, charting the rims in his heavy engineer's shirt, knee breaches, high-laced boots, sweater, cap, and necktie. After his death, a 7,800-ft. high peak on the north rim was named in his honor.

The beauty of the Canyon was not always a stimulus for painting. William Allen White contributed to the railroad's extravagant *The Grand Canyon of Arizona, Being a Book of Words from Many Pens*. In its 1909 edition, White wrote this account of one of these unnamed artists:

> Once an artist who loved the wilderness brought his bride to the head of the Bright Angel Trail. . . . She looked out across the miles and miles of tumult of form and riot of color that seemed to swirl thousands of feet below her and around her. As from the clouds she looked down into an illimitable red tinged, ash-colored hell, abandoned and turned to stone aeons and aeons ago, she stared amazed at the awful thing for a long minute, and then, as the tears of inexplicable emotion dimmed her eyes, she turned and cried vehemently to her artist husband: "If you ever try to paint that, I'll leave you."

The Santa Fe capitalized on the famous artists' paintings. In 1903, the railroad purchased Bertha Dressler's *San Francisco Peaks*, which Dressler had painted in 1900 on a trip to Flagstaff; the painting memorialized that trip. In 1907 alone, Simpson acquired 108 paintings. Shortly thereafter he purchased and reproduced as a postcard Frank Paul Sauerwein's painting *The First Santa Fe Train Crossing the Desert*. In 1905, the railroad agreed to sell his works at El Tovar. After his death at the early age of thirty-nine, his ashes were scattered on the Painted Desert.

In all, the railroad acquired more than six hundred paintings of the Canyon from these well-known western artists. These artistic reproductions of the majesty of the Canyon may well have played a decisive role in making the Grand Canyon a national park. In 1917, for the National Park Conference in Washington, D.C., Stephen Mather arranged what he called a "First Exhibition of National Parks Paintings," at the National Gallery of Art. There were 45 paintings exhibited. With the cooperation of the Santa Fe, 16 were of the Canyon, which was not then part of the national park system. These 16 Canyon paintings included works by Leigh, Daingerfield, Potthast, Walter, Ufer, and others whom the railroad had brought to the rim to paint the Canyon. Thomas Moran himself had two canvases.

Mather was a prime mover in this exhibition; he considered it, in part, a chance to persuade Congress of the propriety of making the Grand Canyon a national park. The exhibition was a rousing success. Within less than two years, Congress designated the Canyon a national park, and Mather found himself as the newly named director of the National Park Service. Mather Point at the main automobile entrance to the Canyon honors his work today. The memorial overlooking the Canyon there concludes: "There will never come an end to the good that he has done."

THE AMBIANCE ALONG THE RAILS

Train crews on the rail line did not always feel enthusiastic about the Canyon line. True, the scenery in places could be magnificient, especially in the fall and in the snowy months of winter. Unlike many other railroads, the tracks ran through neither slums nor junk yards. But the right-of-way was not fenced. The tracks traversed miles of open range where wild animals had the right-of-way. Often they loitered on the tracks and would not move. Sometimes trains could not stop in time. The nimblest—deer and antelope—were rarely a problem, but sheep, cattle, and wild burros often would not move. In a collision, sheep caused the greatest problem: wool and tallow would roll up and impair air lines to the brakes, making it difficult to stop.

Some engineers were saddened while others were proud of hitting animals. While throttling through Red Lake in December 1907, S. O. Miller, one of the line's famed engineers, saw a majestic black-tailed deer running ahead of the engine. Suddenly it turned, darted across the tracks athwart the engine, and was instantly killed. Miller, along with the passengers and crew, lifted the dead animal onto the engine. He continued to the station with the carcass draped across the engine. Later the hide and head were mounted and the antlers put on the front of the locomotive. For years Miller boasted of being the only deer hunter in the West who chased and captured his game with a locomotive.

CONNECTIONS WITH THE MAIN LINE

In its heyday the Canyon railroad carried dignitaries, politicans, miners, cowboys, ranchers, and thousands of ordinary tourists from all over the world. One of the more illustrious, President Teddy Roosevelt came to the rim via the rails in 1903. He arrived at the rim and took a horse to Grandview, where he stayed overnight at the Grandview Hotel. On May 6, from the hotel balcony, he gave a speech, which, among other things, thanked the Santa Fe for deciding, according to him, not to build a new hotel on the rim. Even as he spoke, however, the railroad was completing plans to build the massive El Tovar hotel right on the same rim.

Deeply moved by the grandeur of the Canyon, Roosevelt declared his visit there "the greatest day of my life." He then delivered sentiments which are often quoted:

> I hope you will not have a building of any kind, not a summer cottage, a hotel or anything else, to mar the wonderful grandeur, the sublimity, the great loveliness and beauty of the Canyon. Leave it as it is. You cannot improve on it. The ages have been at work on it, and man can only mar it. What you can do is to keep it for your children, your children's children, and for all who come after you as the one great sight which every American . . . should see.

Roosevelt must have liked the Canyon; after his 1903 visit, he returned again in 1911 and took an extended hunting trip to the bottom, with John Hance as his guide.

At its peak in the 1920s and 1930s, passenger traffic was so great that the railroad ran up to three special sections in the summer. To accommodate this traffic with the greatest comfort, the railroad arranged its schedules so that passengers on the fast transcontinental trains between Chicago and Los Angeles could get to the Canyon with minimal inconvenience.

One of the Santa Fe's crack Pullman trains, the California Limited, arrived in Williams from Chicago at 10:45 P.M. Pullman cars routed to the Canyon were switched from the Limited onto a siding. Cars returning from the Canyon switched onto the Limited and travelled on to the coast. Canyon-bound cars left Williams with a fresh engine at 5:30 A.M. and arrived nonstop at the rim in time for breakfast. Passengers could thus sleep in their Pullmans throughout the night and arrive for breakfast at El Tovar for a full day of sight-seeing without any interruption. At 8:45 P.M. the night train left the Canyon and arrived in Williams at 10 P.M., where its cars switched onto the Limited for the trip west. In the mid-1930s, the fare for this round-trip event was a mere $7.60.

The railroad's promotional material about the trip to the Canyon repeatedly praised the smooth connections in Williams. This material assured passengers that they would have a pleasant trip that, in the railroad's words, would be "a novelty and delight." Railroad brochures reminded passengers that the roadbed to the Canyon, unlike the main line, was laid with heavy steel and ballasted with marvelous lava cinders, which made for an unusually smooth ride.

But the ride did not always match these glowing descriptions. In the mid-1930s, English humorist writer J. B. Priestly travelled to the Canyon with his family. They made the connection in Williams from the Limited. Priestly's description of the connection found no place in the railway's promotions:

> We had planned a "stop-over" of a few hours. Your coach leaves the main westbound train in Williams, Arizona, wanders up the 64 miles to the station at the southern rim of the Canyon, doing this during the night when you are fast asleep, and when you awaken in the morning—there you are.

For the Priestly party the reality did not quite match the advance promotions. He continues his account:

> The night that had seemed very convenient and comfortable in the railway timetable was actually most unpleasant. First there were giant shuntings and bangings that made sleep impossible. By the time I had adapted myself to these shuntings and bangings they stopped, and the train was left paralyzed in an uneasy silence and stillness, a doomed train that whispered "sleep no more." In the end I must have slept a little, for I remember waking to find that we were somewhere very high and it was snowing.

Despite the loss of sleep caused by the "shuntings," Priestly nonetheless was enthusiastic about the Canyon and the trip to it. In his famous essay in *Midnight on the Desert* [1937], written shortly after his visit, he wrote eloquently of the Canyon in the vein of Teddy Roosevelt and Santa Fe passenger agent C. A. Higgins:

> The Colorado River made it, but you feel when you are there that God gave the Colorado River its instructions. It is all Beethoven's nine symphonies in stone and majestic light. Even to remember that it is still there lifts up the heart. If I were an American, I should make my remembrance of it the final test of men, art and politics. I should ask myself: Is this good enough to exist in the same country as the Canyon? How would I feel about this man, this kind of art, these political measures, if I were at that Rim? Every member or officer of the Federal Government ought to remind himself, with triumphant pride, that he is on the staff of the Grand Canyon.

AMBIANCE AT THE STATIONS

Both at Williams and at the rim, the arrival and departure of trains generated enormous excitement and activity. One reason for the excitement was the trains themselves, with their lordly names—the California Limited, the Missionary, the Scout, the Pioneer, the Super Chief, El Capitan, the Chief, the Grand Canyon. Passengers on these elegant palaces peered out from their windows with all the finery and sophistication of supposedly superior big Eastern cities, and in return Harvey Girls, cowboys, "dudes," and assorted frontier folk stared back from rustic station platforms. Starched Harvey Girls at the Williams and Canyon stations stood primly in the background to give advice on food and lodging. Harvey drivers lined up at the depot offering rides to hotels. Young men shouted through megaphones for tour companies. Baggage carts rattled along the platforms in Williams and at the Canyon as luggage shunted from train to train and to hotel jitneys. Hissing and banging filled the air as steam engines and coaches uncoupled and shunted about.

Prior to 1919, the editors of *The Saturday Evening Post*, vocal advocates for making the Grand Canyon a national park, often criticized this disrespectful scene. To the *Post* this "leather-lunged yawp for trade" right at the rim was an outrage to the sacredness of the place. The *Post* regularly editorialized that this irreverence had to stop.

Billy Bass, John Muir, and David Steele may have described the train-Canyon interplay more accurately or, at least, more softly. Muir visited the Canyon shortly after the first train arrived in 1901. In an essay in *Century Magazine* in 1902, he reflected on the difference between what he had expected and what he actually observed:

> When I first heard of the Santa Fe trains running to the edge of the Grand Canyon of Arizona, I was troubled with thoughts of the disenchantment likely to follow. But last winter, when I saw those trains crawling along through the pines of the Coconino Forest and close up to the brink of the chasm at Bright Angel, I was glad to discover that in the presence of such stupendous scenery they are nothing. The locomotives and trains are mere beetles and caterpillars, and the noise they make is as disturbing as the hooting of an owl in the lonely woods.

After visiting the rim in 1917, David Steele wrote a book about his trip entitled *Going Abroad Overland: Studies of Places and People in the Far West*. He too noted the presence of the trains, writing that "beyond the station there are miles of sidings where [there are] long trains of solid Pullmans, four, five or six sections to one schedule, each one with two engines, equipped to haul two thousand persons in or out per day."

Steele noted that, in his view, the Canyon "had arrived." Every day, he observed, there detrained "notables from all four quarters of the habitable earth," who climbed the steps to the rim where they were rendered "speechless" or even "fainted or prayed." Like Muir, he described the interplay between the trains and the Canyon:

> The first and possibly the most astonishing thing the travellers to the Grand Canyon experience is the fortunate nature of the approach to it. There is absolutely nothing to appraise you that the place is nearer than a million miles until you step out of the train right at its edge, almost right

into it. A hole more than a mile deep at the side door of a railroad station and hotel which you have entered from an absolutely level course across the desert . . . The train comes to a sudden stop. And you are at the gate of heaven.

Canyon guide Billy Bass also wrote compellingly of the romance at the Canyon and at Williams engendered by the hustle of the trains and excited passengers. Unlike that of *The Saturday Evening Post,* his description paints a softer and warmer picture. In Williams at the Fray Marcos, lorry drivers, uniformed and polite, waited to meet trains. Passenger agents attended arrivals and departures of sleek streamliners. At the other end of the line at the Canyon, a long line of Fred Harvey Pierce Arrows stood ready at the depot with uniformed drivers in long leather dusters, waiting to take passengers along leisurely rim drives. Starched Harvey Girls stood at the doors of Bright Angel Lodge and El Tovar to greet hotel guests. In the evenings, as the sun sank into the stony West, drivers and girls strolled along the rim and under the porticos at the Fray Marcos and along the porches of El Tovar. If it were a weekend, there would be a dance at Rowe's Well or at the community hall for Harvey Girls, drivers, passengers, and travel agents.

As Bass solemnly reminded his readers, behind every scene there loomed the omnipotent yawn of the chasm as the majestic screen on which all these human scenes played. As he concluded, one could not be more fortunate than to live and work at the Canyon in such halcyon times.

6
Mary Jane Colter and Canyon Architecture

AS THE SANTA FE RAILWAY pushed west and opened restaurants and hotels to accommodate its and the nation's growth, it found that it needed not only a Fred Harvey as its hotelier but also its own architect to design its facilities. An Irish schoolteacher from St. Paul, Mary Jane Colter, filled this role both for the Santa Fe and for Fred Harvey. In 1902, she began a career that led her to become their architect, designer, and decorator. Her work for both masters contributed indelible and unique artistry to the Canyon, whose south rim structures constitute her biography in stone.

Colter was born in Pittsburgh in 1869. In 1880, her family moved to St. Paul, where she became fascinated with western Indian culture. At a turn-of-the-century vacation in San Francisco with a friend working for the Harvey Company, she commented that she, too, would someday like to work for Harvey. Her friend passed the word. Shortly thereafter, she received a telegram from Harvey offering her a part-time job arranging handicrafts at the depot gift shop in Albuquerque.

From this modest beginning, Colter gradually worked herself up to the position of draftsperson/designer of Harvey buildings along the vast Santa Fe system. Although hired by Harvey, she was also employed by the railway. Harvey operated the restaurants and hotels of the railway but owned only the furnishings. The railroad owned the buildings and land. The railroad needed someone to design passenger-related facilities in its buildings, which, after completion, would be turned over to Harvey for management.

For more than three decades, Colter served these two masters in her role as architect. She also met her own demanding standards for exalting native peoples and preserving the natural environment by building structures of indigenous materials. Her central task for the Santa Fe Railway and the Harvey Company was to submit designs for exterior and interior construction. Harvey would initially approve or disapprove her designs, which, after approval, were passed onto the Santa Fe for implementation.

Hopi House

When Colter first came to work part-time for her masters in 1902, her first task required her to become well informed about southwestern Indian culture. The Santa Fe told her that the Grand Canyon especially needed a decorator "who knew Indian things and had imagination." The railway gave her an initial construction project at the Canyon: an Indian building adjoining El Tovar.

Hopi House, as this new structure became known, was built immediately east of El Tovar, where it still stands today. The Hopi Indians had inhabited the area for centuries; they once had a cluster of primitive structures near El Tovar. Colter wanted her building there to resemble the rock and adobe pueblos of the Hopi living at Oraibi, one hundred miles southeast, where in 1540 Hopi guides had conducted Coronado's men to the rim. The building was also to serve a commercial purpose as a salesroom for Harvey's Indian arts.

Colter drew up designs unusual for her day. The building was made of stone and wood native to the area. The rocks came from the Canyon itself, and its wooden beams were harvested from the surrounding forest. The levels of the building were intentionally irregular. Wooden ladders gave outside access to higher floors. Stone steps and wooden ladders connected one rooftop to another, and each roof served as the porch of the apartment above it.

The building was not to be just a commercial complex for Indian arts but also an Indian dwelling. Colter insisted that Hopi artists be given a chance to live in the upper floors, which they did for several decades.

The building's interior reflected the same Hopi style as its exterior. Massive adobelike walls of plaster were fashioned to appear like a haphazard collage of rock and mud. Ceilings were constructed of ponderosa log beams with smaller pine branches crossing at angles. The cement floors appeared as native rock and mud. Hopi baskets, blankets, and pottery sat about the walls and halls. In the corner of one room, Colter designed an impressive Spanish fireplace, with its mantel exhibiting Hopi religious figures and candlesticks. Other rooms incorporated a Hopi altar and unusual sand paintings.

Colter sent her designs to the Harvey Company and then on to the Santa Fe office in Los Angeles. Making minor changes, both approved her plans. Construction began in 1904. Hopi Indians did much of the labor. Two days before Hopi House opened, the Hopi held a private dedication ceremony, to which Colter was the sole non-Indian invited. Hopi House opened almost simultaneously with El Tovar in January 1905.

The strategic location of Hopi House directly east of El Tovar allowed rail passengers easy access from El Tovar and the depot. Passengers spending only the day at the rim could easily detrain at the depot, visit Hopi House, and dine nearby at El Tovar before returning on the night train to the main line. Hopi House symbolized the partnership between commercialism and romanticism that came to characterize Harvey and Santa Fe advertisements.

All Hopi House wares were on sale on the outside patio at 5 P.M. daily. At the same time, Indian groups sang and danced, finishing up a short time before departure of the southbound evening train. To the Santa Fe Railway and the Harvey Company, a tourist visit to Hopi House was not only an exercise in commercialism but also a discovery of new peoples, new artifacts, and new life-styles so different from the urban East. The Santa Fe's effusive *Grand Canyon Outings*, published in 1936, even assured curious tourists that the Hopi living and working at Hopi House were "industrious, thrifty, orderly and mirthful."

In 1910, when Colter was forty-one years old, Harvey and the Santa Fe offered her a full-time job. Her success at the Hopi House played a part in the decision. Her task from this point on was to do full-time what she had done so well with the Hopi House: design and decorate hotels, restaurants, and station facilities for Harvey and the railway throughout the vast Santa Fe system. Her formal title comprised the dual roles of architect and designer. She continued to be paid both by Harvey and the Santa Fe but now had the luxury of having other architects working directly for her.

Hermit's Rest

After designing station facilities for the railroad in Lamy, New Mexico, Colter returned to the Canyon and redirected her energies to the Canyon's needs. Tourism was sprouting. The railroad delivered thousands of passengers each year to the rim. Some wanted to view the Canyon from along its dramatic western rim, which lacked both access and facilities. In 1912, the Santa Fe built the present west rim drive, which it first called the Hermit Rim Drive. The Harvey Company began running sight-seeing tours along the rim but there were no facilities to serve as a terminal or rest stop for these trips. A terminal was especially needed at the end of the long eight-mile drive on the west rim. Passengers needed a midway rest and viewing spot before returning to the village. Hermit's Rest, Colter's next project, was designed to meet these needs.

Hermit's Rest derived its inspiration from the hermit Louis Boucher, who lived near that site from 1891 to 1912. Known to early Canyon denizens as the Hermit because he was a quiet person who rarely came to town to mix with locals, Boucher sported a white beard, rode a white mule with a large silver bell, and usually carried with him the tools of a prospector. Some said of him, unfairly, that he wore a white beard, rode a white mule, and, unlike John Hance, told only white lies. His name and roots were French-Canadian. He had come to the Canyon originally as a trail guide. Like Hance, Bass, and others, once he arrived he found he could not leave, even if staying meant living without steady work other than guiding and hosting.

Boucher's eventual home at Hermit's Rest consisted of tents and a small corral for horses and mules. His trail, which began at Rowe's Well, led to a large orchard of peach, orange, and fig trees, plus a vegetable garden of tomatoes, cucumbers, melons, and grapes. This trail led eventually down in the Canyon to his two-tent, one-corral tourist camp one mile from the river. Because of his solitary ways and his majestic white mule, white beard, and soft-spoken nature, he became known only as the Hermit of the West Rim.

Blocked access to the Bright Angel Trail by Cameron, the Santa Fe in 1911 built the "Hermit Camp" at the bottom of the "Hermit" Trail, which it named after Boucher. This camp offered rustic tourist cabins, a corral, and dining hall. Although the buildings are now gone, faint outlines of these structures are still visible today. The Santa Fe wanted to accommodate west rim tourists, to be sure, but it also intended that the trail and camp compete with Cameron's Bright Angel Trail.

The railroad constructed the west rim road leading to Hermit Trail in 1914. In its celebratory booklet entitled "Hermit Rim Road and Trail" [1915], the railway called its Hermit Rim Road "the most famous drive in the world," modestly adding that it was "the most unique scenic roadway in the world."

Colter's task on the Hermit road was to live up to this grandiose billing by memorializing the man, his hermitage, and the rim road. In 1914, she designed a small stone terminal that was one-story tall to avoid competition with the dramatic surroundings. The building was primitive in every respect. Harvey and the Santa Fe liked the design. The entry traversed an arch of stones randomly piled near the entrance. Under the doorway she hung a broken mission bell acquired from the station in Lamy, New Mexico. From one of the projecting stones in the wall she hung an old iron lantern as a beacon shining for the homeward hermit. The structure incorporated stones and boulders from the immediate area, as well as natural logs cut from nearby pines and piñons. The front porch extended to the edge of the rim, and only a low stone wall separated tourists from the yawning chasm. Furniture had this same rustic design; sofas and chairs were even built of tree stumps and logs.

The point of attention inside the building was the stone fireplace perched under an archway within an even larger stone arch. A large, facelike stone protruded from the fireplace above its hearth. In front of it, Colter placed an open-mouthed bear rug. Windows on the Canyon side permitted those inside to sit by the fireplace and gaze out into the chasm. Upper-level windows added celestial light to overcome the stony darkness. A devotee of iron, Colter added touches of it in strategic places: a candelabra, metal lanterns, old andirons, and door hardware.

Hermit's Rest cost Harvey and the Santa Fe $13,000, a meager sum for such an unusual rest house. Harvey tours on the west rim stopped here beginning with its opening in 1914. Hostesses served passengers tea, crackers, and cookies without charge. Colter prided herself on the ancient look of the building. She responded to critics by saying "You can't imagine what it cost to make it look so old."

The railway celebrated the completion of Hermit's Rest and the Rim Road with its laudatory publication entitled *Hermit Rim Road and Trail* [1915]. In its enthusiastic pages the railway described the building as "like a hermit's cave of prehistoric times" and added that the structure was "a resthouse unlike any other in the world."

The Lookout

Simultaneously with the construction of Hermit's Rest, Colter was designing another Canyon structure—the Lookout. The Lookout related to the nearby Kolb studio in somewhat the same way as El Tovar related to Cameron's original hotel. Indeed, the Kolb brothers and the Camerons had much in common, including formidable enemies.

The Kolb brothers, Emery and Ellsworth, had arrived at the Canyon in 1901 with photographic equipment that they had purchased in Williams. Emery arrived first, making the trip by train; Ellsworth walked the tracks all the way from Williams to mile 52, where he hailed a northbound train and rode in style, cheaply, for the last twelve miles.

In 1904, the brothers, with Cameron's approval, built a frame, two-story building just below the rim alongside the Bright Angel Trail, at a point where Cameron's tollgatherers collected tolls. In 1902, Cameron allowed them to put their photography studio on rim property next to his hotel. In 1904, again with Cameron's approval, the brothers' two-story building just below the rim became a concession of its own, for Cameron allowed the brothers to take pictures of trail hikers at the exact spot where they paid their tolls.

The Kolbs soon developed their building into a photography studio where, for a fee, they permitted tourists to enter, take pictures, buy film, and view their spectacular photos of the Canyon. The Kolbs also worked closely with Cameron by taking pictures of hikers as they entered—and paid for—Cameron's trail.

The Kolbs resembled their friend Cameron in other respects as well. As part of their program of dramatic river photos, they lectured their audiences on the evils of the Santa Fe Railway, park management, and the Harvey Company. In their building on the rim, they also conducted activities inappropriate for such a dramatic location: they had a soda fountain overlooking the chasm and conducted Wednesday night dances with booming music. On Saturdays they showed movies with loud soundtracks. They had plans for a pool hall overlooking the rim. Later, they found a human skeleton in the Canyon, which they brought back to their building and showed to select audiences.

The Canyon master plan of 1917, not surprisingly, described the Kolb building as "unfortunate both as to design and location" and concluded that it did not belong on the rim. But, like Cameron, the Kolbs had no intention of moving from their prized location.

Harvey and the Santa Fe preferred that tourists not be charged for looking into the Canyon and taking pictures of it. The Lookout became the answer to the Kolb problem. Colter was told to find a spot for a competing, free photography structure. She found a promontory jutting out over the Canyon even more dramatically than did the Kolb studio. She designed a structure to fit the dramatic pinnacle. On its porch she placed telescopes. Inside she designed a small studio where viewers could purchase film, photos, unusual rocks, scientific books, and pictures.

Its exterior continued the rustic tradition of the Hopi House and Hermit's Rest: a one-story, irregular-roofed building of Kaibab limestone piled haphazardly to resemble Hopi dwellings. Its chimney appeared as a random pile of stones of the same type as the background Canyon wall. Colter succeeded in making it blend so perfectly into the limestone of the rim that it drew no attention away from the Canyon.

Again the Santa Fe celebrated its completion with a promotional publication. In its 1915 tourist brochure, the railway described the Lookout as "built like an eagle's eyrie." In a self-congratulatory but accurate footnote, the railway noted that, except for the Bright Angel Trail, which charged a toll,

> all the other modern facilities for getting around the Grand Canyon have been provided at great expense by the Santa Fe Railway for free use by the public. A systematic development of roads and trails now makes it possible for visitors to see the most interesting sights easily in comfort. Hermit Rim Road and Hermit Trail were wholly built by the Santa Fe at an expense of over $100,000. Thousands of dollars also have been spent by that company in improving and maintaining the roads to Grandview, Desert View and Yavapai Point; and in fixing up the Tonto, Dripping Spring and Waldron Trails; likewise many pathways have been opened up through the woods on the rim.

In its 1936 *Grand Canyon Outings*, the railroad boasted that the Lookout even served as a "quaint observatory."

Phantom Ranch

After World War I, tourists travelled to the Canyon in large numbers. Passengers on the Canyon railroad increased from 44,000 in 1919 to more than 100,000 in 1923. Many wanted to descend into the chasm to stay overnight at the very bottom. Those who did usually could not make it back the same day, which meant either curtailing the descent or sleeping under the stars. With park service encouragement, Harvey and the Santa Fe decided to build rustic accommodations at the very bottom midway between the north and south rims, to serve as an overnight facility for those who braved the trail to the bottom.

An early trail down the north rim had been developed by David Rust in 1902. In 1903, he and E. D. Wooley created the "Trans-Canyon Transportation Company" to improve a rim-to-rim trail. Although these trails existed from the early 1900s, accommodations at the bottom at Rust's Camp were practically nonexistent. In 1905, Rust set up a permanent hunting camp at the junction of Bright Angel Creek and the Colorado River. In the fashion of the day, he called it his "camp." Four years later, like Bass, he built a tramway sixty feet above the river to allow hunters to cross the river via a cage attached to a cable. Theodore Roosevelt visited the camp in 1913 and took this crossing; his visit caused the camp's name to change from Rust to Roosevelt.

Communication between the north and south rims was a further problem. From the time El Tovar opened, there was no way to communicate between the rims. For a time between 1910 and 1920, the Harvey transportation manager used a fire to signal "Uncle Jim Owens" on the north rim that guests would be hiking to the north rim via the Bright Angel Trail. Such methods, however, were not always successful.

Early tourists could reach the depths of the Canyon via either the Bright Angel Trail or the Hermit Trail. Both trails reached the river, but the Bright Angel Trial was almost directly in line with the primitive trail to the north rim, whereas the Hermit Trail was miles to the west. The Bright Angel alignment seemed the most appropriate for an overnight facility. The park service built an original suspension bridge in 1921 that offered easy and dramatic access to the north bank near the Bright Angel Trail. Although there were trails and a bridge, there was still no place to stay.

To Colter, this river crossing suggested that the ideal location for an overnight facility was under a grove of cottonwood trees along Bright Angel Creek about a mile north of the suspension bridge. In 1932, she designed not just a single facility but a small community—a group of small stone cabins surrounding a central dining and recreation area, which offered rest, food, and communications with both rims.

On the west border of the site, Colter found river-worn stones, which she used for the foundation and walls. Larger uncut river rocks were also used for the walls. They measure a couple of inches in diameter to a couple of feet and give the buildings a chunky, bulbous look. Wood and metal materials travelled laboriously down the trails on the backs of mules.

Each cabin was funished with rustic beds, a desk, and a chair, plus a fireplace and Indian rugs. The central building—a kitchen-lodge—was of the same format but larger. It offered a commodious kitchen for cooking plus a dining area capable of serving seventy-five hikers. Colter placed a large recreation hall designed in the same wood and river-rock design just south of the dining hall, and located a swimming pool, now removed, just to its north side.

Colter named the small community Phantom Ranch after nearby Phantom Creek, a tributary of Bright Angel Creek, upon whose banks the Anasazi Indians had grown squash, corn, and beans a thousand years before. The name is appropriate not only because of the creek but also because of the misty battlements uptilted over the site.

The Santa Fe Railway again celebrated Colter's triumph in print. In a brochure issued in 1932, the railroad announced "a new inter-canyon oasis, recently built on the east bank of Bright Angel Creek in the bottom of Bright Angel Canyon." It continued:

> There are accommodations available in stone cottages built of colored canyon boulders.... It makes possible evenings and nights in an atmosphere of unreality thousands of feet down in the heart of the earth.

Shortly after its opening in 1932, Phantom Ranch acquired its lasting reputation as a small exclusive resort for the intrepid and long-suffering who hiked or rode mules the 5,000 vertical feet down to it. Its location 9.5 miles below the rim gave it a deserved reputation for isolation and solitude—traits it still bears today.

The Watchtower

The site where the Canyon had first been seen by Coronado's men was near Desert View, some twenty-five miles east of the present Canyon village along the east rim drive. That road had been first built by the railroad in 1912. In the 1920s and 1930s, Fred Harvey coaches were taking tourists along this drive. As with the west rim drive, Harvey and the Santa Fe needed a terminus for this trip where tourists could disembark, stretch their legs, peer into the Canyon, and learn something of the area. Again Colter received the task to design an appropriate terminal.

In her mind the ideal structure would be not only a functional rest stop but much more: a memorial to the Hopis who lived nearby and to the Coronado explorers they had led to this site for their first view of the Canyon. Nearby Colter discovered her plan in the ruins of an ancient Hopi lookout tower. For many months she researched and sketched different kinds of Hopi towers. From these sketches she made a small, tablesize model complete with trees and shrubs. The site chosen was directly on the rim near the place where Coronado's expedition first viewed the Canyon in 1540.

The tower was to be a "re-creation," to give rebirth to the archetypal Hopi tower whose ruins were scattered in the area. The structure was built primarily of native stone collected from the rim, with large wooden timbers carved from nearby ponderosa and piñon pines. She decorated the interior with cave and wall drawings copied from nearby Hopi dwellings, plus petroglyphs copied from those on rock walls in the area. The interior sported a gift shop situated in a Hopi ceremonial chamber known as a *kiva*.

Near the junction of the Colorado River and the Little Colorado, Colter came across a circular spring that the Hopis called *sipapu*, or "entrance to the underworld." According to Hopi beliefs, human beings emerge at creation and return at death through the sipapu. A Hopi kiva is a hole in the ground symbolizing a sipapu. Ancient ruins of such sipapus have been excavated near the Tusayan museum. Colter decided, in light of these discoveries, that the walls of the massive rim structure would illustrate both a sipapu and a kiva.

The resulting structure was seventy feet tall, thirty feet at its base. It had a well-disguised concrete and steel support system.

Its interior steel circular framework was designed and built by the Santa Fe's bridge department. On the outer surface near the entrance to the stairway Colter inserted into the wall a grotesque, irregular stone, which, with some imagination, resembled a Balolookong, the great plumed serpent of the Hopis. The kiva portion of the structure illustrated how a kiva was used: there was an entrance through the roof, with a ladder descending as far as the log ceiling, and nearby was an altar that served as the center of religious and social activities. The ceiling was constructed from logs salvaged from Peter Berry's original Grandview Hotel.

The center of the Watchtower was the Hopi Room. On its walls Colter and her Hopi associates painted the story of the Snake Legend and the legend of the first man—a Hopi—to navigate the river through the Canyon. On the second-story walls and ceiling, Colter and her Hopi artist Fred Kabotie placed designs for the God of Germination, the Star Priest, and the God of Little Wars. Part of the ceiling showed stars and constellations.

On its west exterior, Colter built a ruin to resemble how Hopi watchtowers appeared when they were first seen by non-Indians—a pile of large boulders capable of being mounted but seeming to tumble down. She studied ruined Hopi towers in the area before designing this portion. Its location gives an accurate idea of the kinds of ruins archeologists still occasionally find in Hopiland.

Colter named this, her most unusual accomplishment, the Watchtower. The name commemorated many things—ancient Hopi defensive watchtowers, the Hopi watch for the dead and the afterlife, the sipapu legend, as well as the Coronado expedition's first view of the Canyon from near this site in 1540.

After three years of careful construction, the Watchtower was dedicated May 13, 1933, in a Hopi religious ceremony. Dancers and Hopi priests blessed the structure and distributed piki bread to the audience. The blessing gave Harvey and the Santa Fe excellent publicity; it was covered by hundreds of newspapers and radios and even filmed for Paramount Pictures.

The Watchtower still commemorates not only these native

and historical values but also the artistic skill of Colter and her respect for the naturalness of Hopi tradition and place.

Bright Angel Lodge

Increasing rail traffic at the south rim required more lodging and dining facilities. El Tovar could not meet tourist needs for the great numbers visiting the Canyon on holidays and the summer season. Harvey, the Santa Fe, and the park service saw the need for a new hotel. The original depot yards provided the location.

At the turn of the century, the area around the original depot was called Bright Angel Camp. It sported the rough and decrepit Bright Angel Hotel first built by stagecoach owner J. W. Thurber, plus a cluster of cabins and a collection of army-style tents that rented for $1 a night. Well after the railroad's arrival at the rim, the Santa Fe purchased the original Bright Angel Hotel for use as rustic tourist lodgings. The railroad's attention, however, was taken up with tourist facilities at El Tovar rather than at the Bright Angel area. By 1935, the hotel was showing age and neglect, and the area surrounding it was disorganized and often trashy. Colter was commissioned to design something more fitting to the scene.

She first had the original hotel demolished. She wisely avoided the temptation, popular with some, to demolish all the original structures in the camp. She insisted that Cameron's Hotel—the Red Horse Stage station and, later, the Canyon's post office—be preserved, as well as Buckey O'Neill's cabin, still perched on the rim.

Her original design for a new hotel was not approved, probably because it was perched so close to the rim as to prevent pedestrian traffic. She then designed a pioneer-style building compatible with the rustic Cameron Hotel and O'Neill cabin, one story in height, with massive wooden beams and a discreet use of stone for walls and floors. The Santa Fe's Chicago office architect drew the final plans and awarded the contracts.

The resulting Bright Angel Lodge consisted not only of the new lodge but also of the historic cabins adjacent to it. The Cameron Hotel was saved not only for its historic significance but also for its hand-squared construction. The Santa Fe purchased it from the park service and Colter then made it into one of the Bright Angel cabins. Buckey O'Neill's rim cabin also became part of a 17-room guest lodge she added west of the new lodge.

Bright Angel Lodge itself was a large stone building with a sweeping, high-pitched roof. Its front porch had massive log columns supporting equally massive log roof beams. The south entrance door facing the railroad tracks led into a large lobby of stone floors and log ceilings. Antique lamps decorated outside and inside entrances. At the north side of the lobby sat a massive open-hearth fireplace with stone benches on either side where hikers and others could warm themselves. Above this fireplace Colter placed a dramatic wooden thunderbird, the Hopi symbol for the powers of the air. The Harvey Company had adopted this symbol for its Indian Detour trips some twenty-five years before. To Colter the thunderbird also represented the "bright angel" that greeted and protected Canyon visitors.

Behind and to the west of the lobby, Colter designed a smaller, more intimate lounge. Its two large windows framed the Canyon yawning just outside. Between these windows she constructured what she called the "geological fireplace," another massive stone structure whose stone layers correspond in sequence and kind to the layers of stone comprising the Canyon outside the window. River rock from the bed of the river forms the hearth of the fireplace, and Kaibab limestone, the Canyon's top layer, constitutes the topmost layer of the fireplace.

At the opening of the lodge on June 22, 1935, two thousand people came to the celebration. Hopis, Navajos, and Supis came from distant reservations. Indian dances, cowboy songs, and a ceremonial banquet with leaders of the park service, Harvey Company, and the Santa Fe helped dedicate the new structure.

The Super Chief

One of Colter's final projects indirectly touched the Canyon but was not permanently located there: the design and decor for the Santa Fe Super Chief. First conceived in 1936, that train was to be a fast diesel streamliner carrying only first-class Pullman passengers. It hauled five Pullmans, a diner, lounge, and dome car. It accommodated 104 passengers in exclusive sleeping quarters, plus a train crew of 12, and offered nighttime connections with the Canyon line at Williams. The Santa Fe intended this to be its premier streamliner, the most luxurious train in America. To that end every car was to exhibit authentic native American decor taken from western sites.

Colter borrowed the names of each of the Pullmans from Indian pueblos along the Santa Fe route. Each was decorated with Indian sand paintings and murals showing southwestern themes. For the table service in the dining cars she borrowed a design taken from thousand-year old Mimbres Indian pottery unearthed along the New Mexico-Arizona border. The pottery survived by its unusual use at funerals, where a decorated bowl was "killed" by making a hole in its bottom and then was placed on the deceased's head to allow spirits to enter and leave.

By the mid-1930s, Colter and her Indian associates found enough "killed" and whole pieces of pottery to suggest thirty-seven different patterns. Most of these are stylized designs of living forms corresponding to water, sky, and land. Mimbres china typically exhibits birds, animals, and fish within a cosmic border.

Because of its origins this china became called "Mimbreno" after the Mimbres Indians. Its use on the *Super Chief* reminded passengers of the traditions of the ancient natives of the Southwest. Like other elements of the train's interior, Colter's china adapted Mimbres likenesses without sacrificing the simple honesty of the original design. Mimbreno China was used exclusively on the *Super Chief* and its Canyon connection from 1938 to 1971. Since then it has become a rare and highly valued collector's item.

Mary Jane Colter died in 1957 at age eighty-eight, appropriately in Santa Fe, New Mexico. Her forty-six years of sevice with her dual masters had by then been filled with lasting successes unique to herself and to the Canyon. Of all the places she designed for the Santa Fe and the Harvey Company, the Grand Canyon was her favorite. It had the greatest number and, in her view, the best examples of her work. Colter Hall, an employee residence west of El Tovar, memorializes her name and her work at the Canyon.

Today, six of her most dramatic structures still stand on or near the rim: Hermit's Rest, the Lookout, Hopi House, Phantom Ranch, Bright Angel Lodge, and the Watchtower. With their devotion to natural materials, Indian symbols, and surroundings, these unusual structures catch the spirit of the land and the people with which they blend so well. Her rustic style even entered architectural annals: it became known as "National Park Rustic," an environmentally-blended style copied by the national park system throughout the West well into the 1950s.

7
End of the Line

BY 1929, THE PROPORTION of tourists at the Canyon favored the automobile over the train by a 2:1 ratio. On June 9 of that year, in order to increase ridership with easy Canyon connections, the Santa Fe initiated a new through-service train called the Grand Canyon Limited. Advertised in omnipresent Santa Fe promotions as a "no extra fare train," it allowed Pullman passengers to make a side trip to the Canyon without leaving main line coaches. When its westbound consist arrived in Williams at 4:30 A.M. through sleepers and coaches shunted onto train No. 14 of the canyon line, which left Williams at 5:20 A.M. and arrived at the rim two hours later. At 8 P.M. that night, southbound train No. 5 left the Canyon. On its arrival in Williams at 10:20 P.M., its through cars switched to a siding until the Limited arrived at 4:30 A.M., whereupon the sleepers switched onto the Limited and left Williams at 4:50 A.M. for the West coast.

This schedule continued in one form or another until 1964. That year through cars dropped from the Limited and moved to train No. 17, the combined Super Chief/El Capitan, for westbound traffic and to train No. 20, the Chief, for eastbound traffic.

In the 1930s the Canyon line worked hard to survive. In addition to passengers, it carried livestock and sheep to ranchers along the way, particularly to Quivero and Valle. It carried logs from Apex at milepost 52, where the Saginaw and Manistee Lumber Company operated a logging camp between 1928 and

1935. Trains also delivered mail and water to ranches along the way. Until 1936, its tank cars delivered all the Canyon's water from Del Rio, 120 miles south of the rim. By 1931, railroading was the fourth most important industry in Williams; fifty families there were entirely supported by the Santa Fe payroll.

ROAD AND AUTO COMPETITION

In Ralph Cameron's time, two auto roads served the south rim—one a dirt road from Williams, the other the old stage route from Maine, now called Parks. In the mid-1920s, the park service repeatedly sought authority and funds from Congress for a paved road to the rim. It regularly entreated Cameron's replacement, Sen. Carl Hayden, to support an appropriation in Congress for that purpose.

After a number of unsuccessful efforts, the park service decided to invite Hayden to visit the Canyon to see firsthand the need for such a road. Hayden agreed to come and see for himself if such a road was needed.

Well versed in the useful aspects of the summer monsoon, wily park service officials arranged in the summer of 1928 for Hayden to drive the Maine road to the Canyon during the very time when summer monsoons made it a bog. Hayden's entourage was mired axle-deep several times along the Maine road. Shortly after his return to Washington, D.C., the park service found that it had received funds for a paved highway from Williams to the rim. In improving the Williams road to the rim, the park service thereby unwittingly succeeded in doing what Ralph Cameron had tried and failed to do: hasten the departure of the railroad from the Canyon.

The new paved road was very popular. By the mid-1920s, rail travel to the south rim only slightly exceeded auto traffic. By 1927, auto travel exceeded rail travel for the first time. The figures never changed. By 1930, the automobile far surpassed the railroad in tourist volume to the rim. In 1932, as rail ridership was being overtaken by the auto, the Santa Fe reduced its daily round-trip trains to the rim from two to one.

The railroad tried a new, short-lived experiment in the early 1940s. The El Tovar, listed as trains 123 and 124, began operation between Los Angeles and Kansas City via the Canyon as a summer supplement to the Grand Canyon Limited. The next year the route was shortened to provide service between Los Angeles and the Canyon. El Tovar was the only Canyon train to use open-platform observation cars. It terminated in 1942.

With the outbreak of World War II, the railroad suspended passenger service to the Canyon in July 1942 for the duration of the war. A bus operated in the interim. Freight, water, and livestock continued by rail. A legal change also occurred: the "Grand Canyon Railway Company," the nominal legal entity, was dissolved, and its property and name became incorporated into the Santa Fe.

Motive power to the rim remained as steam to 1950. The first diesels appeared as early as 1938, primarily for publicity purposes. Diesels made their first regular appearance in the 1951 schedule. In March 1952, the Canyon line became entirely diesel-powered. Heavy passenger cars ran until 1956, when lightweight coaches first appeared. In that same year, the Santa Fe discontinued service before May 25 and after September 30, in silent recognition that the line was used almost entirely by summer tourists.

In 1961, the railway completed a relocation of its main line track around Williams on the town's north side. The result was that main line trains no longer used the Fray Marcos station in downtown Williams but a new, smaller station at Williams Junction, three miles to the east. Timetable directions for Canyon trains strangely changed as well: train No. 14 southbound from the rim was described as "eastbound," and No. 15 northbound became "westbound."

The Williams downtown station continued to service Phoenix-bound trains, but Canyon and high-speed main line trains used the Williams Junction station. The Junction station lasted only eight and a half years. At its peak, it was the busiest station between Denver and Los Angeles, serving as many as fourteen passenger trains daily, including the Canyon runs. All that remains today of the Junction station is a concrete slab.

END OF THE CANYON LINE

After World War II, the railroad's former Canyon service of one round-trip train per day resumed. Passengers continued to prefer the automobile. In 1950, rail travel declined a full eight percent from the prior year, while total tourist travel to the Canyon almost doubled.

By 1960, ridership declined to 10,000 annual passengers. By 1967, it had fallen to 4,658. On April 25, 1968, the Santa Fe notified the Arizona Corporation Commission that it intended to discontinue all passenger service to the Canyon. In May, the commission determined that passenger service was still "reasonably necessary." The commission ordered the railroad to resume service on May 26, 1968. The Santa Fe appealed. In July of that year, the Arizona Supreme Court allowed the railroad to discontinue passenger service immediately. At 5:30 P.M. on July 30, 1968, No. 14 left the Canyon depot for the last time with one baggage car, one lightweight coach, and three revenue passengers. Passenger service ended when the train arrived in Williams.

In 1969, the railroad petitioned the corporation commission to terminate freight service. The commission granted the request. On May 16, 1969, the railroad closed its Canyon station and the next month its station at Williams Junction. Freight service, principally unscheduled lumber, cattle, and sheep, continued on an irregular basis until November 1, 1972. The last Santa Fe train on the line was a work train in the summer of 1974 that removed sidings and switches and demolished many trackside structures. The Canyon line became only a fond memory.

The demise of the line left behind majestic gravestones, notably El Tovar and the unique depots in Williams and at the rim, which served as reminders of grander days. Built to service rail passengers, El Tovar seemed especially lonely. Physically and historically linked with the Canyon rails, it now seemed to be suffering a divorce from its mate.

After 1974, the rails were visited only by juniper and pine trees, which began to sprout in great numbers in the railroad's once-proud, high-grade ballast. By the 1980s, ponderosa pine trees were growing between the ties.

8

Re-inaugurating the Rails

AFTER THE FINAL PASSENGER train left in July 1968, successive investors made sporadic efforts to resurrect the line. The initial efforts, although unsuccessful, helped prepare the way for the effort that did succeed.

EARLY EFFORTS AT REVIVAL

Some of the early efforts to revive the Canyon line involved major personalities. On September 29, 1977, radio and TV personality Arthur Godfrey visited Williams along with Don Prenovost and three members of the incipient Grand Canyon Railroad Development Company. Their visit involved inspecting the Fray Marcos and the roadbed. Godfrey's interest in the project was as promoter and investor. His group had plans for a museum, depot, and roundhouse in Williams.

Initial negotiations began with the Santa Fe for purchase of the track. In October 1977, Godfrey withdrew from the project because of family problems. The interest of the other members of the group waned. The tracks continued to sprout trees.

In March 1981, the Santa Fe filed a notice of intent to abandon the track. That announcement spurred a private group, the Canyon's Railway Company, to organize and purchase the entire right-of-way for a price tag exceeding three million dollars. Within two weeks, the contract was scratched because an important California investor failed to secure financing. His associates returned to San Francisco and left the tracks to generate more rust and vegetation.

In 1984, hopes rose again. A Phoenix company named Railway Resources under the leadership of Charles Newman tried again. In April of that year, for an amount in excess of $3.2 million, the company acquired the tracks. In May, Newman put the project on hold pending difficult negotiations with the city of Williams for purchase of its water reservoir from the Gonzales estate on the northeast side of town.

With this hurdle behind him, Newman waxed enthusiastic about his plans. He announced that the company would be hiring workers in the next months to replace some 20,000 ties and to clear vegetation and trees from the roadbed. In October 1984, he announced financial commitments to complete the line. Railroad sources expected major international investment. It hoped to sign the final papers for financing in December 1984. Newman even predicted an expected opening by July 4, 1985, in time for the Olympics in Los Angeles.

Little happened to match these rosy predictions. No news came from company offices in Phoenix. No work on the line was visible. By July 1986, Railroad Resources had paid only $1.2 million of its debt to the Santa Fe. To save the plan, both parties worked out a restructured contract. Under its terms, Railroad Resources would take ownership of only the very northern one-third of the line and would tear up the southern two-thirds of the track and deliver it to Williams, where the Santa Fe would recycle the rail. In return, the Railroad Resources debt to the railway would be cancelled.

Railroad Resources was unable to meet even these modified conditions. The Santa Fe then repossessed forty-four miles of track at the southern end of the line, while Railroad Resources retained control over the northern twenty miles.

The date of March 11, 1987, was a cliff-hanger for Williams and the Canyon line. National Railroad Constructors, Incorporated, of Phoenix, hired by the Santa Fe to remove the rails, sent a work crew to Williams with instructions to tear up the tracks to Anita. As the first spikes were being pulled, word spread around Williams of what was happening. In a western-style confrontation consistent with its turbulent history, Williams city marshal John Moore appeared on the scene, holstered, and he served legal papers on the president of the company. These papers cited him for operating without a city license and for demolishing without a demolition permit. Moore impounded the two spike-pulling machines. National's crew rode out of town—until later, undiscovered, they reputedly sneaked back onto the line at milepost 6, well north of town, where under cover of dusk they hastily removed two rails that they brought back to the Santa Fe as proof of at least partial success.

THE NEW CANYON RAILROAD

The successful revival of the Canyon line began on July 7, 1988, when Max Biegert, a Phoenix businessman who had invested in Newman's project, announced his purchase of the northern portion of the line from Railroad Resources. Instead of scrapping the tracks and recouping his losses, Biegert hired a California research company of ex-Disneyland officials to do a feasibility study. That research indicated that the Canyon railroad had great potential. Biegert then actively sought financing. Undaunted by the reluctance of banks to issue such large loans, he collaborated with his father, two brothers, and others, plus a group of private investors, to raise $15 million to put the new venture on solid footing.

Biegert's first impulse was to restore the line only from the rim south to Tusayan, some ten rail miles. The Tusayan terminus in his view would serve that town and the Canyon airport, as well as auto traffic on highways U.S. Route 180 and Arizona 64. But the city of Williams continued its tradition of belligerence. It reminded Biegert of its propriety and historical interest in the railroad and of its status as Gateway to the Grand Canyon. Williams also reminded Biegert that a terminus in that town would enable the railroad to draw passengers from Phoenix, Amtrak, and Interstate 40. Biegert and his advisors saw the wisdom of refurbishing the entire line.

In the fall of 1988, he took possession of Newman's assets—a pile of studies, reports, and plans, the northern twenty miles of tracks, plus bad feelings generated by fifteen years of frustration, and began restoration of the Canyon rails. He first repurchased the southern forty-four miles of track and right-of-way, plus some private land at Apex at milepost 52, four miles west of the Canyon airport. He decided to defer the airport service for several years so that all finances could be directed toward the success of the longer route from Williams.

Biegert and his group invested $5.4 million merely to buy the tracks and adjoining real estate. An additional $12 million was used for construction, renovation, and other start-up expenses. In all, $80 million was needed. In January 1989, at a press conference at the Grand Canyon depot, he announced that the rebuilt railway would begin operating in April 1990.

REPAIRING THE ROADBED

The original roadbed, first graded in 1899 and 1900, was built with compacted clay and volcanic cinders. Between 1907 and 1909 the Santa Fe found it necessary to pull up much of this track and rebuild the roadbed because of the instability of the original construction. By 1974, after the last track maintenance, many of the ties had rotted. Within a few years of neglect the roadbed had eroded and was sprouting vegetation. By 1984, piñon and ponderosa pines were growing between the rails, especially at the northern end of the line. Some trees were almost a foot in diameter.

The new railway marshalled its road crews at milpost 5 north of Williams on March 28, 1989, and began putting together what vandals and the weather had torn up. They inspected 275,000 ties and marked an *X* on those needing to be replaced. Bridge beam replacements and abutment work were also necessary. In some areas, especially near milepost 6, new rails needed to be installed. Roadbed crews were followed by bridge crews who worked in areas where the roadbed had already been refurbished.

In early summer the new company purchased two diesels for road work—ex-Santa Fe GP-7s, No. 2072 and No. 2134, which had seen roadway work for the Santa Fe in Texas. From June 22, 1989, these diesels hauled carloads of volcanic cinder ballast up and down the line from the loading area at milepost 8 near the original pit that had furnished the first cinder ballast in 1906. The six hundred gondola loads of cinders were deposited directly on top of the ties and then swept between them to keep the ballast level with the ties.

On July 3, 1989, road crews entered the Grand Canyon Park to address substantial problems there. Large pine trees between the rails needed to be removed, and some tracks needed straightening and levelling. Crews also had to remove roots and asphalt, replace ties, improve grade crossings, and install crossing signals.

The roadbed in narrow Coconino Canyon just south of the rim needed special attention. The rails there run through an ancient canyon with steep walls and a meandering wash. Over the railroad's eighty-eight year history, flooding and derailments had occurred here. The banks along the rails needed to be stabilized and culverts restored to carry runoff away from the roadbed.

By the time roadbed work was completed in late summer of 1989, seventy-seven laborers had inspected 275,000 ties and had removed some 30,000 of them. Six hundred carloads of cinder ballast had been used to shore up the roadbed, and some steel rails had been replaced. Bridge beams and abutment repairs totalled almost $1 million.

PASSENGER EQUIPMENT

None of the original passenger coaches used on the original Canyon line was appropriate for the new railway. The lightweight coaches used in the line's later years lacked nostalgia; the original heavier coaches had either disappeared or were in disrepair. The railroad therefore sought and eventually bought a series of coaches of 1920 vintage. They fall into two classes. In January 1989, eleven clerestory coaches were purchased from the Central New Jersey Railroad. These coaches are seventy-two feet long and seat a maximum of seventy-eight passengers. The second, larger group of coaches were built by Pullman Standard in the early 1920s and had previously been in use on Southern Pacific's San Jose-San Francisco commuter line. Each is a Harriman coach, eighty feet long, with ninety-two reversible seats and concrete floors.

All the coaches were restored at the Pacific Fruit Express car shops in Tucson or at the railway's shops in Williams. Each required sandblasting and repainting. The interiors were restored with green plush seats of velour and mahogany. Floors and walls returned to their original colors. Art Deco photos and ads were installed at the ends of the coaches to create a 1920s atmosphere.

DIESEL LOCOMOTIVE POWER

On March 29, 1989, the railroad purchased its first two diesel locomotives from the Santa Fe. Delivery was made to the company tracks on April 23. Both are GP-7s of the 2650 road switcher class, manufactured by General Motors in 1953. The Santa Fe rebuilt them to their present configuration in the early 1970s. Their last service with the Santa Fe was in Texas. Their duties on the Canyon railway include hauling ballast cars and ties and acting as backup to the steam engines.

STEAM POWER

In June and July 1989, the railway purchased four steam locomotives from private individuals. All are 2-8-0 consolidation engines. Three of the four are SC-4 class locomotives of consecutive serial numbers—18, 19, and 20. All three were built in 1910 by the American Locomotive Company (ALCO) works at Schenectady, New York. The fourth, No. 29, is a SC-3 class built by ALCO in 1906 in its Pittsburgh shops. All four were completely rebuilt by the Presque Isle shops in 1930. The fourth steam locomotive, No. 29, had been displayed in North Freedom, Wisconsin, before arriving in Williams in August 1989.

Service for all locomotives from their manufacture to 1960 was with the Lake Superior and Ishpeming Railroad in Michigan. They hauled iron ore trains twenty miles from Ishpeming to the Marquette ore docks. Locomotive No. 19 had seen service as a scenic railroad in the Marquette area. All locomotives arrived in Williams on flat cars.

They needed general repairs and specific attention to boiler repair, running gear rust removal, replacement of boiler insulation, and conversion from coal to oil. The tender cars that originally carried coal were converted to carry oil, a cleaner and less polluting fuel. "Gray Water"—reclaimed effluent—is now used for the boilers. All the repairs for these engines were done at the railway's shops in Williams.

Another steam locomotive, Burlington 2-8-2, No. 4960, was purchased in August 1989 from Mid-Continent Railway Museum in Wisconsin. It is a heavy Mikado 2-8-2 whose small drivers are ideally suited to the roller-coaster profile of the roadbed. No. 4960 had been used in the 1960s for steam excursions on the Burlington railroad. It was called "the Teacher" because of the school children it hauled in the Chicago area.

Shortly after purchasing and refurbishing the engines, the railroad purchased and rehabilitated an unusual railcar—a Jordan spreader, a large plowlike railcar capable of plowing snow from the tracks and spreading cinder ballast on the roadbed.

THE RE-INAUGURAL RUN

The very first train to the rim had arrived September 17, 1901. By accelerating its work schedule by several months, the revived railway completed restoration of the roadway and equipment well in advance of the originally announced opening in April 1990. In mid-summer 1989, the line's directors announced that the first train under the new regime would leave Williams for the rim on the exact date of its ancestor eighty-eight years before, September 17.

Achieving this goal required enduring some unexpected events. For one thing, the steam engines had to be converted from steam to oil. The designated lead-off engine, No. 18, did not arrive in Williams until August 20, three weeks before its scheduled departure. It had to be rebuilt, repaired, and repainted. Crews worked on No. 18 until 1:30 in the morning of the re-inaugural departure.

Other dilemmas arose. The railway had invited some seven hundred dignitaries and travel agents as guests on the initial run. That number of people required seven passenger coaches. Even with its best upgraded boiler, No. 18 could only haul five coaches. The company decided to attach the two diesel engines to the back of the seven coaches not only to help push but also to be ready in case of unexpected problems.

It was a wise decision. After a blessing from a local Navajo Indian and a re-christening before five thousand spectators at the Fray Marcos depot, No. 18 departed on schedule at noon on September 17, hauling seven coaches, with the two diesels at the rear. The locomotive managed to pull its coaches across the high desert at about 35 MPH but developed problems as it neared Anita at milepost 45. It lost its water capacity and suffered the indignity of having to receive a fresh load from a conventional water truck at milepost 45, while the passengers, including Arizona's governor, sat for forty-five minutes admiring the barren wastelands of what the Santa Fe Railway had once called the Black Forest.

When No. 18 finally resumed, it could climb the steep ascent north of Anita only under the pushing power of the two diesels at the rear. When it finally limped into the Canyon depot, it was well behind schedule and had suffered the further indignity of a broken bearing, which made it impossible to pull the coaches back to Williams. The two diesels moved to the head of the train for the return, leaving No. 18 to sit at the Canyon depot overnight.

In the end, the plusses outweighted the minuses. The inaugural train had made it to the Canyon and back for the first time in eighty-eight years. The roadbed and track hummed almost as pristinely as it had in the early 1900s when the Santa Fe first sung its praises. In 1990, its first full year of operation, the reborn railroad carried more than 100,000 passengers, twenty-five times the number who rode in the last year of the Santa Fe's operation.

9

History and Archeology en Route

THE FOLLOWING PAGES OFFER historic and archeological facts about scenes along the Canyon railroad between Williams and the Canyon, beginning from Williams and continuing north to the Canyon depot.

Mile 0: Williams, elevation 6,767 feet. The original Santa Fe Railway train station is the concrete building with ornate pillars surrounded by the original brick platform. It now houses offices of the Canyon Railway. The west end of the building housed a hotel and dining room in the days of Fred Harvey and the Harvey Girls. The complex was originally named the Fray Marcos after Marcos de Niza, the Franciscan friar who acted as chaplain and pathfinder for the Coronado expedition in 1540.

On the south side of the city of Williams rises 9,264-ft. Bill Williams Mountain. It is named for the legendary guide discussed earlier, whose nonexistent grave at the summit was incorrectly but repeatedly advertised by the Santa Fe Railway in early tourist advertisements for the Canyon line. "Civilizing the Frontier at Williams and the Canyon" describes the early rough-and-tumble history of the town of Williams.

The main line track on the south side of the fencing is the Santa Fe Railway main track to Phoenix via Ash Fork.

Mile 1.5: Canyon-bound trains leave the yard limit, turn north, and pass railway maintenance shops on the east and Williams municipal water pools on the west near the first overpass. After crossing under the I-40 and Santa Fe overpasses, the tracks enter the Kaibab National Forest.

Mile 2: Northbound trains enter dense ponderosa pine forest, the largest contiguous expanse of ponderosas in the world. The forest extends from the Arizona-Nevada border, cuts southeast across Arizona, and enters the western half of New Mexico. The pine trees are used extensively for lumber and building projects of all kinds. Sawmills processing the trees operate in the Williams and Flagstaff areas.

To the east under the pine trees lies Kaibab Lake, one of several snow-fed reservoirs providing potable water for Williams. Almost all of the drinking water for Williams comes from snowmelt.

Mile 3: Williams City airport, elevation 6,563 feet, sits west of the roadbed on a small rise. Charles Lindbergh, the first to fly over the Atlantic, helped to select its site in 1928.

In the forest to the east of the tracks are small, boulder-littered canyons where Coconino Indians once lived. Some of their walls contain petroglyphs, which are rock drawings. The markings were etched by Indians living in the area between the eighth and twelfth centuries.

Mile 4: Dogtown Wash, which had been paralleling the tracks on the east, cuts under the roadbed and joins Cataract Creek on the west. At 182 feet, this wooden pile bridge is the longest on the Canyon line. Flash floods here have caused recurring problems, including derailments and a fatal accident in a washout in 1902. Franciscan Father Garces camped on June 26, 1776, at this creek; he named it *Rio Jabesua de San Antonio,* which roughly translates as "Havasu Creek of Saint Anthony."

Mile 4.5: Sweetwater Crossing. The unpaved road crossing the tracks here is Pronghorn Ranch Road. Its name comes from the species of antelope common in this area. The Kaibab National Forest boundary lies north of this road. Pronghorn Ranch itself is about a half mile west of the crossing.

Mile 6: "Pitt" or "Pittsberg," elevation 6,542 feet, are the two names given this area. The first name may refer to a turn-of-the-century sheepherder named William Pitt who pastured sheep in this area. The latter term derives from a major archeological expedition of that name that did an extensive anthropological excavation here in 1938 under the auspices of the Museum of Northern Arizona and other insitutions.

The archeologists involved in that excavation were studying early Coconino Indian settlements here and trying to identify Coconino traits independent of the neighboring Sinagua and Kayenta tribes. Many pit houses and pottery shards were found. The excavations near the roadbed revealed that the immediate area was extensively populated by Coconinos for a lengthy period prior to the twelfth century. Archeologists found pottery, tools, clay pipes, manos, metates, wedges, axes, mauls, pestles, rubbing stones, abraders, sandstone disks, projectile points, and a variety of hammerstones. The variety of tools suggests the Coconino were involved in a wide range of tool technology, while simultaneously hunting, gathering, and gardening.

Mile 6.5: On the east side of the rails sits the roadbed of a "wye," y-shaped trackage used for reversing trains and also for access to the volcanic cinder pit visible in the gash of the humped mountain directly to the east. This cinder pit furnished the ballast for the original roadbed in 1901 and for its improvements in 1907-1909. The southern leg of the wye joins the main line at mile 6.5; its northern leg joins near mile 7. The ties and rails were removed long ago.

Mile 7: The cinder pits on the southwestern face of the humped volcanic mountain to the east were mined for the Santa Fe at the turn of the century by Chinese laborers using hand shovels. They dug the cinders from this pit and loaded them into gondola cars for use as ballast on the roadbed to the Canyon. The cinders made an especially smooth roadbed. The Santa Fe's turn-of-the-century promotional brochures for its Canyon line repeatedly praised the smoothness of this cinder roadbed and proclaimed that, because of the cinders, the Canyon line "was remarkably smooth," making the rail journey to the Canyon "a novelty and a delight."

Mile 8: Sitgreaves Mountain, elevation 9,388 feet, is the mountain to the east with a series of descending camel-like humps. Its origins are volcanic. Its clay ground cover sits atop hundreds of feet of volcanic cinder, which in turn sits on top of older limestone. The name for the mountain recalls Capt. Lorenzo Sitgreaves, who led an 1853 military expedition to establish a westward route for pioneers moving from Santa Fe, New Mexico, to California. The original Sitgreaves trail extended from east to west just south of this mountain. To the east and behind Sitgreaves rises 10,418-ft. Kendrick Peak, which Sitgreaves named for his military escort.

Mile 9: The tiny hamlet of Red Lake, elevation 6,777 feet, sits east of the tracks. It is so named because of the color of the small volcanic lake just east of Arizona 64. This area has both historic and archeological significance. From 1898 to 1901, as the first rails were being laid toward the Canyon, Red Lake sported a telegraph station and a cattle track, which have long since been removed.

In 1949, archeologists affiliated with the University of Illinois and the Museum of Northern Arizona made a field school expedition to this area to define Coconino culture and address specific questions about their settlements in this area. Red Lake Wash near the tracks revealed remnants of ancient Coconino dwellings. Eleven sites were excavated between 1949 and 1951. Differing kinds of architecture appeared, including circular and elongated pit structures both below and above ground. Several sites had rock check dams that were probably used by the Coconinos to hold back rainwater for irrigation. The earliest Coconino structures in this area appear to have been pit houses partially dug into the ground. Later habitations were built above ground. The 1949 expedition concluded that the Coconino had a distinctive culture separate and apart from neighboring tribes living in the area during the same period.

Mile 11-12: Cedar and Squaw mountains sit northeast of the tracks in piñon and juniper trees. Both mountains, along with Sitgreaves to the south, contain numerous Coconino structures revealing a major settlement here between A.D. 700 and 1100. Evidence for their presence here comes from distinctive red and black pottery, pit houses, and obsidian rock mined from one of the southern peaks of Sitgreaves. Coconino habitations include both above-ground and below-ground houses, as well as enclosed storage areas.

The Coconino made a distinctive gray pottery, sometimes decorated with black, now called San Francisco Mountain Grayware. They appear to have been accomplished stone workers in flaked stone, as shown in their obsidian arrowheads and manos and metates still discoverable in the area. Petrified wood has also been found at some sites here. Since it is not natural to this area, it is likely that it was obtained by the Coconino in trade with Indians further east, perhaps those living in the Petrified Forest area. It is possible that both petrified wood and obsidian, the latter found here in great quantities, were used as trading currency between these sites.

The Museum of Northern Arizona and Oberlin College performed extensive field investigations on the western slopes of these mountains between 1989 and 1990. Among other things they found more than two hundred pit house depressions, attached masonry rooms, plus stone axes, turquoise, animal bones, bone tools, burned corn cobs, and slab-lined kilns—the latter probably used for making ceramics. Examination of shards in the area suggests that Coconino ceramics may have been made at Duck Lake, just south of Sitgreaves Mountain.

Archeological explorations of these western slopes reveal large above-ground masonry sites with massive walls and large plazas. Although the purposes of these rock formations are unclear, their massive size suggests that they may have been used for ceremonial and religious purposes.

The obsidian blanks found in this area appear to have come from one of the smaller southern peaks of Sitgreaves Mountain and possibly also from Government Mountain northeast of the town of Parks. These blanks seem to have been used for tools and for trading with other tribes. Obsidian artifacts from these mountains have been found across the Grand Canyon and as far south as Phoenix, as well as into Colorado and New Mexico, indicating an extensive trade in obsidian currency among differing tribes during the Coconino occupation of this area.

For reasons not fully known, possibly from a prolonged drought, the Coconino disappeared from these slopes about A.D. 1150. This area remained abandoned for some two hundred years until the ancestral Havasupai appeared on the plateau about A.D. 1400.

Mile 13: Laws Spring lies east of the tracks in an arbor of piñon and juniper. The Beale expedition camped here in 1857. Members of the group carved inscriptions on the boulders around the spring. The boulders also contain petroglyphs of Coconino Indians formerly residing nearby, as well as inscriptions from a Union Pacific Railroad survey crew that camped here in April 1868.

Mile 14.9: Beale Wagon Road appears on the east as a one-lane wagon rut and begins to parallel the tracks through juniper and piñon trees. Shortly north it turns west and crosses the tracks. This wagon road was the first federally funded interstate roadway for westward travellers before the construction of the railroad and Route 66. The Beale road was heavily travelled by wagon trains and covered wagons moving west from Santa Fe, New Mexico, during the years 1860-1882.

The area where the Beale Wagon Road crosses the tracks is the approximate location of Bly, a sheep- and cattle-gathering area. Its name derives from the former Fletcher Bly sheep ranch dating from pioneer days.

Mile 15-16: The volcanic cinders that had been the principal ground cover begin to disappear; from here north to the Canyon the surface rock is limestone. The volcanic eruptions to the south covered the underlying limestone formations, which now begin to appear and become dramatically more visible at the Canyon.

Mile 16: To the east of the roadbed lie several high mountains:

Humphreys, Kendrick, and Sitgreaves are the most visible. Humphreys is the tallest mountain in Arizona at 12,663 feet. It is named for Andrew Atkinson Humphreys, the officer of the U.S. Corps of Engineers who evaluated the data from several western surveys and chose the eventual route of the Santa Fe Railway main line through the Southwest.

Mile 16-18: Humphreys Peak, elevation 12,663 feet, rises to the east, with its summit covered with snow for the colder half of the year. In addition to its railroad and scenic history, it also has biological significance. In 1889, biologist C. Hart Merriam led a major scientific expedition to this area and published the results as a theory of "life zones," which became a milestone in the development of the science now called ecology. Here he made the first comprehensive description of western plant and animal life as seen in relation to altitude.

In 1889, he and his researchers made a base camp on the western slopes of the San Francisco Peaks at an elevation of 8,250 feet. From there they made explorations into the Painted Desert to the east and the Grand Canyon to the north. The research, which was focused on Humphreys Peak, led Merriam to define seven life zones running from the top of the mountains to sea level, each with distinctive plants and animals differing from those above and below. Merriam also discovered on these peaks the San Francisco groundsel, a delicate alpine plant found nowhere else in the world.

Like many other scientific theories, Merriam's life zone theory categorizing life in terms of altitude has been much modified since his day. His contribution was not a final answer to the relationship between altitude and life-forms but rather a starting point for later scientific research. His life zone theory appears to be most applicable to the western mountains where his theories originated. The theory survives today as a handy means of relating differing life-forms to differing altitudes and climates. While the generalizations on temperature have been largely discounted, Merriam's research on these mountains remains generally viable and constitutes a cornerstone of the expanding science of ecology. The Merriam elk is named in his honor.

Mile 17-18: Two lakes decorate the area. Over a small ridge east of the tracks sits Smoot Lake, probably named for William H. Smoot, a cattleman living in the area about 1881. Howard Lake and Howard Mesa also lie over a ridge to the east. The Howard name possibly comes from Jesse Jefferson Howard, known as "Bear Howard," a local mountain man and contemporary of Old Bill Williams. Bear Howard is said to have hunted bear with a passion after one killed his ranching partner in the 1880s.

Mile 18-19: Mt. Floyd, elevation 7,439 feet, rises in the distant western horizon. Like Sitgreaves, it was a primary locale for Coconino settlement and obsidian mining. Mt. Floyd obsidian is glassy, black, and comparatively brittle; it differs in color and strength from that found on Sitgreaves Mountain. Its presence here suggests that there was trade in obsidian rock internal to the Coconinos. The exchange of the two kinds of obsidian between these mountains suggests that the Coconinos or their traders may have seasonally migrated from Mt. Floyd to the volcanic peaks further east.

Mile 20: Quivero, elevation 6,035 feet, is the name given this pastoral area. The name is a Spanish corruption of *Quivera,* the name of one of the seven golden cities of Cibola sought by the Coronado expedition that passed near here in 1540 under the lead of Don Lopez de Cardenas. Occasional copper deposits in the area could account for the name as well as for the illusion that there was gold here.

In its heyday in the early decades of this century, Quivero was a large sheep collection and shipment area. Ruins of the old station and animal pens lie east of the tracks.

Mile 26-27: As the northbound train descends into a barren desert, the north rim of the Grand Canyon appears momentarily on the northeast horizon as a thin blue line fifty miles to the north. These are the limestone rock formations of the upper portion of the north rim of the Canyon. They are visible here because of their height; the north rim is some 1,000 feet higher than the south rim and rises above the intervening formations.

Mile 29: Valle, elevation 5,904 feet, is the name for this small settlement of ranch buildings on both sides of the tracks. The road that crosses the tracks here extends east to Arizona 64. The name for the area is the Spanish word for valley. The term is an appropriate name because the area is near the lowest point on both the railroad and highway routes to the Canyon. The buildings along the tracks are the Bar Heart Ranch. On the west side, concrete remains recall the small railroad station here, which, in the early days of the line, was a regular stop. Near the station foundations are the remnants of a thirty-seven-car rail siding used for cattle and sheep loading. Before the Grand Canyon airport was built, the nearby airport at Valle served the Canyon.

The masonry bridge here, fifty feet in height, is the highest bridge on the line. In Spring Valley Wash, just north of the ranch buildings, train passengers can see folded limestone on the east side of the tracks on the north bank of the wash. This horizontal rock stratum was formed when this rock yielded to the same uplifting pressure that ages ago raised the south rim of the Canyon.

This barren and arid area was labelled the "Black Forest" on a Santa Fe Railway route map of 1884, suggesting that its map makers had never explored this area, which probably has never generated anything other than grama grass.

Mile 30-31: Elevation 5,800 feet, lowest altitude on the Canyon line. The tracks descend to the lowest point in a wide, barren depression that 200 million years ago in the Permian period held a great saltwater sea. This area is very dusty in the early summer months, which often generated descriptions of stage passenger discomfort.

Mile 34: Red Butte Mountain, elevation 7,370 feet, a brilliant sandstone peak, is the lonely rock outburst whose cone rises 1,300 feet above the horizon to the northeast. Red Butte was the name given the peak by Whipple in 1864 on his railroad survey south of here. Lt. Beale had been in the area before Whipple, however, and he had named the formation for Lt. C. E. Thornburn, USN, who was in charge of the itinerary report for the Beale expedition. The Thornburn name obviously has not stuck.

Red Butte is visible for many miles. It was a prominent landmark for the Havasupai Indians, who gave it an Indian name meaning "Mountain of the Clenched Fist." There is some suggestion that the Indians considered it a sacred place; ruins suggesting religious rites have been discovered near its summit. Even Beale saw some religious significance in it: on September 15, 1857, he noted its dominant presence and described it as "of curious form, rising out of the plain and entirely isolated . . . the sides quite red above half way up and the shape of the whole somewhat resembles a bishop's mitre."

The mountain sports a cap of basalt that dates from its volcanic eruptions in the Cenozoic era. This hard cap saved it from the wind and water erosion that levelled former neighboring mountains that eons ago were worn down to ground level.

In 1949, the University of Illinois and the Museum of Northern Arizona carried out seventeen major archeological excavations here. Scattered Coconino Indian sites were found in the forested areas south of the butte. Six other sites were excavated in 1951. Significant excavations also occured at Harbison Cave near the butte in 1971. The

1971 excavation of Harbison Cave yielded many obsidian artifacts, suggesting that the cave may have been a Coconino commercial or trading center with obsidian being used as currency and the cave functioning as a bank.

The butte also has some commercial history: the first Grand Canyon airport was located near the base of its north slope, along the old Maine stage road to the Canyon. The airport was used principally in the 1920s. Planes later moved to the larger Valle airport and then to the present Grand Canyon airport.

Mile 36: Miller Wash cuts back and forth under the roadbed. The wash flows northwest when it has water. Its name probably recalls P. C. Miller, a pioneer cattleman whose cattle ran in this area at the time the first rails were being laid. An old passing siding parallels the main line on the east. A fatal wreck occurred on this wash in 1916 as the southbound night train from the Canyon entered this wash in a freak summer hailstorm; the tracks buckled, crushed the tender against the engine, and pinned the fireman against the boiler.

Mile 38: Willaha, elevation 5,900 feet, is probably a Supai Indian word for "watering place." It may also be a corruption of the German word *Valhalla*, the palatial afterlife in Scandinavian and German mythology. The largely Swedish population living at Apex north of here in the 1930s was known to be influenced by Scandinavian and Germanic myths and it is possible, although unproven, that the name comes from that group. There is also a "Walhalla" plateau in the Canyon; its name comes from François Matthes, the cartographer who named many of the Canyon formations for Norse gods and Scandinavian myths.

An old water tank, warehouse, shed, and rock bunk house on the east side of the tracks were built by the Santa Fe Railway in 1919 for the adjoining De Ryder Ranch. The ruins of the original station lie to the east just north of the Willaha Road crossing.

Walhalla Road, which crosses the tracks here, leads to the Havasupai Indian reservation at the bottom of the Canyon. That area suffers severe flooding during heavy rains. In September 1901, in January 1910, and again in the late summer of 1990, flood waters from Havasupai Creek rushed through Supai and forced evacuations. Similar problems occurred during the heavy rains of January and February 1993.

Mile 39: Red Horse Wash, elevation 6,000 feet, is the name given the usually dry wash crossing under the roadbed here. Franciscan priest Francisco Tomas Garces camped here in July 1776 en route to the

Canyon. He named this wash *Pozo de Santa Isabel,* "Spring of Saint Isabel." He was the first white man to meet the Cerbat tribe living at the bottom of the Canyon. On this same trip he gave the Colorado River its lasting name.

Mile 40.5: In the forest several miles east sit the Red Horse and Moqui stage station ruins. These stations served as rest and horse-changing opportunities for stages on the Maine and Flagstaff runs between 1892 and 1901. The stages ceased shortly after arrival of the rails at the rim. The stage stations in most instances were left to decay in the weather. The foundations of the houses and corrals are still visible on the forest floor.

Mile 42: On both sides of the tracks lie mesas containing copper ore. This ore motivated the building of the Canyon railroad. Copper Queen mine sits in these limestone cliffs to the east; it was mined extensively from 1901 to 1905.

Mile 43.8: This nondescript area is called Woodin, elevation 5,930 feet, on railroad maps. Its origins are unclear. It may be a corrupted English spelling of *Wodin* (Odin), the chief divinity in Scandinavian mythology. There is a Wotan's Throne in the Canyon, which received its name from German-educated François Matthes, who named many Canyon promontories after Norse gods. Like Valhalla, the name may have originated with the Swedish immigrant lumberjacks living in the 1930s at the Saginaw and Manistee Lumber Company up the tracks at Apex. The name may also possible refer to W. H. Woodin, the president of the American Car and Foundry Company in St. Louis, which built railroad cars for the Santa Fe as well as other railroads. The name may also refer to Bill Williams' friend and fellow-guide, Dick Wootton, whom the great pathfinder John Fremont sent to retrieve the goods stashed in the fatal snowy pass in the deadly expedition of 1848. Dick Wootton is also memorialized on the Santa Fe main line near Raton Pass, New Mexico.

Mile 45: Anita, elevation 5,920 feet, is the name of the former mining settlement that sat here in the first four decades of this century. A station, section house, and cistern were located here, as well as many small homes of miners who worked the ore mines located at the end of a 2.87-mile spur formerly extending off to the northeast.

In 1899 and 1900, when the tracks ended at this point, Bass stagecoaches met trains here to transport early Canyon tourists the remaining twenty miles to the rim, before the rails reached the rim in 1901. Passenger service to this point began in the spring of 1900, when the

Santa Fe and Grand Canyon railroads issued timecards showing the passenger schedule to Anita.

Anita was a regular stop on the local Canyon train. It was also a mail and cattle stop. The nearby Yeager-Bly cattle and sheep company had a mail and grocery drop alongside the tracks, where trainmen would leave supplies and mail in a tamper-proof pouch. Yeager was a pioneer sheep rancher in the area who sometimes allied himself with Fletcher Bly.

Anita, now a ghost town at best, had more history than any other intervening station stop along the Canyon line. Its name comes from Tom Lombard, one of the principal investors for the Canyon railroad, who named the site for his daughter in 1897, when the original line was being planned.

The arrival of the rails here in 1900 spurred extensive mining in the area. These mines were the prime motivator for building both the Canyon main line and the spur heading off to the northeast to Anita Camp. The scattered ore still to be found in the surrounding mesas prompted mining by as many as thirty-one companies from 1890 to 1910. The mines extended over some six miles; most were located in Rain Tank Canyon Wash just northeast of the tracks. Their names reflect great expectations—Copper Prince, Copper Queen, Copper King, Anita Queen, After Thought, Commodore Dewey, Eastern Star, and Grandview were among the more prominent.

As many as twenty families lived here until 1940. An ore smelter sat where a sidetrack left the main line at Anita Junction. An ore loading ramp built in 1918 still sits east of the tracks and south of Anita Road, which crosses the tracks here. The ramp and smelter were used by several copper miners, notably Peter Berry, who built the Canyon's Grandview Trail.

The roadbed of the spur track to Anita Camp was built in 1898; its remains are still visible off to the east as it ascends into the piñon pines along the limestone cliffs containing the ore. Some trackside structures still sit, collapsed, alongside the original roadbed. At Anita Camp, stone and wood foundations of miners' turn-of-the-century homes dot the forest floor, which is still cluttered with rusting tin cans, bottles, shovels, and occasional ore cans and buckets. Excavated entrances to the original mines sit on both sides of the old roadbed. The roadbed of the spur was graded in a gradual descent from east to west, so that loaded cars of ore could be rolled down the rails to the junction at Anita simply by the force of gravity.

Mile 46: On the left is the long-abandoned corral of the Babbitt Brothers Trading Company, which for many years in the early part of this century brought authentic Indian crafts to the Canyon for both the Indian and the tourist trade. The Babbitt family includes among its descendents President Clinton's current secretary of the interior.

Mile 46-47: Rain Tank Wash lies off to the east. Piñon and juniper trees reappear in greater numbers as the tracks ascend the steep geological uplift that formed the Canyon's south rim. After his arrival in Arizona, stagecoach magnate Billy Bass first worked a cattle ranch here. He discovered the Grand Canyon by chance as he was chasing stray cows northward through this wash.

Mile 50: *Hopi* is the name given this one-time station whose name recalls the Anasazi Indians who lived here about A.D. 1200. Some archeologists consider them to be ancestors of the modern Hopi. Hopi Indians at one time lived not only here but also further east along the Canyon's south rim, notably at the Tusayan Ruin not far from Grand Canyon Village, near the spot where Coronado's 1540 expedition reached the Canyon. The Tuysayan Pueblo east of here attests to some Anasazi living on the south rim of the Canyon in the twelfth and thirteenth centuries.

Mile 52: Apex, elevation 6,605 feet, is the name for this now-vanished lumbering community. The name reflects the belief, apparently held by some railroad contractors, that this area was the highest point on the Canyon line between Williams and the Canyon. In fact, the south rim of the Canyon is higher. Apex has retained its name perhaps for another reason: it sits at the top of the long, three percent climb beginning at Anita eight miles south.

In 1928, the Saginaw and Manistee Lumber Company, headquartered in Williams, located a field community here one mile east of the main line. The company began large scale lumbering operations in 1929. With the help of the Santa Fe Railway, the company built and maintained extensive trackage through the forest, including an 85-car wye and spur, double tracks and a 27-car siding, and some 26 miles of track cutting through the forest to the east. The families living here were mostly, although not exclusively, Swedish immigrants whose breadwinners made their living cutting and loading felled ponderosa pines onto railroad flatcars. The cars brought the logs to Apex, where the Santa Fe hauled them to the Saginaw sawmill in Williams. The timber was used, among other things, for railroad ties, railroad track buildings, and for some tourist facilities at the Canyon.

The small community here lived in both traditional houses and railroad freight cars converted from railroad use to domestic purposes. Supervisors enjoyed more spacious homes. Some of these houses were substantial enough to warrant their move to Williams in the 1940s after the Apex community dissolved. In its heyday, the town had only the bare essentials. In 1929, there was a one-room schoolhouse here, as well as a small meeting hall.

After 1935, most lumbering operations ceased; a few years later the railroad removed the tracks. The interested hiker today can follow the original roadbeds through the forest by car; several of the present forest roads follow the original roadbeds. Most historic relics have disappeared, but the careful observer can find some foundations of old structures, as well as occasional rusting pots, pans, and cans scattered under the now-regrown forest.

Apex is in the process of acquiring more railroad history: the Canyon railroad is extending a spur line from this point eastward through the forest to the passenger terminal at the Grand Canyon airport some three miles to the east, with the intention of providing passenger service between the airport parking areas, the terminal, and the Canyon depot on the south rim.

Mile 53: Tusayan, elevation 6,000 feet, is the name given the considerable village lying several miles east of the track along Arizona 64. The name comes from the Hopi name *Tusqua*, given by the Hopi to their original lands here. There is some evidence that the Anasazi Indians lived in this area between A.D. 700 and A.D. 1200.

Located on the east rim of the Canyon, the Tusayan Ruin has a small museum describing the history of the area. The Tusayan Pueblo located nearby was excavated in the 1930s by archeologists; it is now thought to have been home for some twenty Hopis.

About A.D. 1200 the Anasazi left this area and moved to lower elevations to the east. Some archeologists think the Hopis are their modern descendents. The Hopis played a major role in the European discovery of the Canyon; Hopi guides led the Cardenas expedition twenty miles along Hopi salt trails to the rim of the Canyon in 1540.

Mile 55: Coconino Canyon and Coconino Wash, elevation 6,411 feet, meet in this narrow cut between limestone walls. The wash lies principally to the east of the roadbed. A limestone wall at times hugs the west side of the tracks. Coconino and Anasazi Indians lived in the limestone caves visible to the east side of the tracks.

The roadbed here is serpentine. Two horseshoe curves occur almost back to back where the wash twice cuts under the tracks. In the early decades of this century, the curves and the steep 3.22 percent grade were considered so demanding to railroad engineers that the Santa Fe Railway built a simulated section of this portion of the route as a training exercise for novice engineers. It was said in railroad lore that an engineer who could successfully negotiate these curves through Coconino Canyon could handle anything on the entire Santa Fe system.

During the two years before the rails reached the south rim, the rails ended here. Rail passengers were met by a Bass stagecoach, which carried them on their final leg to the rim. The Bass stage trail is still visible; it is the single-rut dirt road crossing and re-crossing the roadbed from the Coconino Canyon bridge north to the Canyon's rim.

Mile 57: Limestone rock ledges decorate the east side of the canyon. Coconino and Anasazi Indians lived in these ledges between A.D. 700 and A.D. 1050. Shortly north are remains of the original railroad station and house for a railroad section crew that maintained the tracks. A bed of a passing track lies in dark cinders to the east. Ruins of another section house with an outside cistern can be seen west of the tracks. The wood and pile bridge at mile 57 crosses over the original Bass Trail, which Bass used from 1899 to 1901 to transport tourists from trains to the Canyon's south rim.

The tracks here follow the beginnings of the Bright Angel Fault, which runs through the limestone formation. This fault forms the small canyon of the roadbed. It extends north to the rim, where it expands dramatically. The tracks from this point on follow the fault to the rim. At the rim the Bright Angel Trail generally follows this fault down to the Colorado River.

Mile 57.8: About midway between mileposts 57 and 58, the roadbed makes an eastward turn in a limestone cut now named Tooker Cut, after an early engineer on the line. On the night of July 27, 1939, the first of several southbound trains took this curve too fast, left the track, and partially derailed, with the engine coming to rest leaning against the limestone wall on the west. The boiler on the engine burst, sending white steam into the moonlight sky, which served as an unexpected but effective warning to following trains to stop before reaching the curve. Fifty-one persons were injured in this accident but there were no fatalities.

Mile 58.5: Hilltop Crossing is the name given this junction of the tracks and Kaibab Forest road 328, which crosses the tracks here en route to the original Bass Camp and Havasupai Hilltop on the Havasupai reservation to the west. The forest road leads eastward to Moqui Lodge, a historic lodge at the entrance to Grand Canyon National Park. *Moqui* is a Hopi word for "vanishing"; it may refer to a group of Hopi who settled here apart from the rest of their tribe. Early maps of the area show a primitive Moqui trail moving east to west north of Flagstaff.

The original Bass stage trail again meets the tracks here, crossing and re-crossing it several times. From 1905 to 1911, Billy Bass's personal railroad depot sat on the west side of this crossing just north of the tracks, primarily to serve the tourists headed for his Bass Camp, twenty-five miles to the west. The station also served as a private residence for the Bass family. It sported a one-car siding for passenger coaches so that Bass Camp tourists could wait there for the next train instead of waiting in the Bass home. Remains of the house and the spur are still visible with careful inspection.

Mile 59: North of milepost 59, the ascent through Bright Angel Fault becomes steeper. Trains slow to 10 MPH. Sanford Rowe's three turn-of-the-century mining claims sit on the west side under the trees. His original Highland Mary claim is the residential structure under the trees on the west side. At the turn of the century, Rowe used that claim to mine and process ore. More recently the structures have been used as employee housing for the Western Gold and Uranium Company.

Mile 60: Dense ponderosa forest crowds the tracks. Early tourists were much taken by the drama of the forest here. From early 1899 to 1901, the tracks ended near milepost 61. Passengers changed to a Bass stage for the final leg to the rim. The track reached the rim in September 1901. The Bass stage road is to the east of the tracks.

The southern boundary of the Grand Canyon National Park crosses the tracks near milepost 60. The train roadbed parallels Bright Angel Wash, which flows alongside the tracks in the geological fault of the same name.

Mile 61: "Rowe Well" or "Rowe's Well," elevation 6,681 feet, is the name given the well and former cluster of hotels and recreation buildings once located at this site by Sanford Rowe, a pioneer stockman and stagecoach guide. In June 1890, Rowe was told by "Big Jim Gwetna" [Vesner], the then-chief of the Havasupais, that water could be found here. With Big Jim's help, Rowe inspected the area and dug a well, where he did pump enough water to help support the ensuing small hotel, campground, and tourist lodgings he located here. These facilities eventually ceased to serve tourists and became the recreational area for Canyon employees between 1910 and 1919. The buildings were removed after this area was designated part of the National Park Service in 1919. Rowe's Well on the west side is also the origin of the Boucher or Hermit Trail into the Canyon, which began here and led to Boucher's home at Dripping Springs.

In summer months, Big Jim's Havasupai Indians formerly frequented this area, where they often camped alongside the tracks in tents and lean-tos in the early decades of this century. Part of their motivation in living here was to gain close access to tourists. Some Havasupai commuted seasonally between this spot and Havasupai Village.

The Havasupai leader Big Jim was a character of sorts. He was supposedly born at Indian Gardens within the Canyon, some 4.5 miles down from the rim, at an unknown date near 1870, well before the arrival of the white man at the rim. In an interview for a guidebook in 1940, he recounted how his parents travelled to Prescott to verify Indian rumors that there were people living there who had white faces. The majestic old chief had a penchant for finery. His formal wear included a frock coat, top hat, and World War I medal given him by the queen of Belgium. He often wore this regalia as he strutted about among his tribe camped here. He regularly posed in this outfit for passing trains.

Mile 62: Maswick Lodge appears under the trees on the east side of the tracks. This lodge originally began as an auto lodge for the Canyon. At mile 62.7, the "yard limit" for the Canyon depot begins, meaning that trains must maintain a slow speed because of possible congestion.

Mile 63: Bright Angel Fault and Lombard converge here. As the train begins a gradual curve to the east, Bright Angel Fault, which the tracks had followed, continues directly north and opens dramatically to the Canyon. Thomas Lombard, one of the original Chicago investors in the Canyon line, dictated that this area would be named after him. His self-imposed name has not stuck.

As the train rounds the curve, there is a fleeting view of the Canyon opening dramatically where Bright Angel Fault meets the Canyon. One of the first small structures on the north side is the former Red Horse Stage station, now a tourist cabin in the Bright Angel complex. This structure was used from 1896 to 1901 as a stage stop on the Flagstaff and Maine stage lines to the rim. It was then located in the forest about fifteen miles south of the rim, some twenty miles east of its present location. In 1901, when the stages ceased operating, Ralph Cameron dismantled the structure and moved it piecemeal to its present site, where he reconstructed it and added a second story. He opened the structure as his Cameron Hotel in 1902 to cater to train passengers disembarking at the then-nearby depot. He also intended the hotel to serve hikers descending his Bright Angel Trail (which he then called the Cameron Trail), which led to his camp near today's Indian Gardens. After Cameron's departure, his hotel became the first post office for Grand Canyon Village.

To the east of this building and adjoining Bright Angel Lodge is the original Buckey O'Neill cabin, the one-story log and mortar structure whose north side opens directly on to the rim. Rightfully honored as the founder of the Canyon railroad, O'Neill built this cabin in his prospecting days as a base of operations for mining and exploring. It is now owned by the National Park Service and is available for rental.

Bright Angel Lodge is the large structure immediately east of O'Neill's cabin. It replaced the original Bright Angel Hotel built by stage operator J. W. Thurber in 1896. Mary Jane Colter designed and built the present lodge, which opened with much fanfare in 1935.

Mile 64: The Grand Canyon depot sits on the north side at an elevation of 6,875 feet at the end of the tracks. The station is the rustic log cabin-type building directly below El Tovar Hotel. Immediately east of El Tovar is Mary Jane Colter's Hopi House. Immediately west of El Tovar is Colter Hall, an employee dormitory that was named in her honor.

The present depot is the second in the area. An early board-and-batten depot sat in 1901 south of Bright Angel Hotel near the wye, approximately a half mile west. The Santa Fe moved its depot to the present spot in 1908 to attract passengers to El Tovar rather than allowing them to detrain near Cameron's competing hotel near the original depot.

The depot is the only log cabin station on the Santa Fe Railway and is reputed to be the only one in this style in the world. It is built of stained pine intended to match its companion, El Tovar Hotel, which is built of Oregon pine cut into half-log veneers.

At the end of Santa Fe passenger service, the depot was deeded by the Santa Fe to the National Park Service and has become a part of the Grand Canyon historic district. It also is listed on the National Register of Historic Places. The park service and the Grand Canyon railway have restored it to the way it looked when it first opened without, however, the brash crowds of tour guides, lorry drivers, and other hawkers cajoling passengers toward waiting buses and lodgings.

Passengers who walk from the depot up the stairs to El Tovar will note on its northside doorway the inscription "Dreams of Mountains as in their Sleep they brood on Things Eternal." Santa Fe passenger agent C. A. Higgins penned these words at the turn of the century for El Tovar prior to his premature death.

THE RAILROAD AND THE CANYON

The awesome view into the Canyon from El Tovar has railroad significance. The cluster of green cottonwood trees 4.5 miles down the rim is Indian Gardens. When Congress in 1895 authorized the building of the Canyon railroad, it specified that Indian Gardens was to be its northern terminus—a feat still thankfully impossible.

Epilogue

There is a dramatic connection between the railroad and the Canyon's environment. Annual ridership on the line averaged 91,000 in its first year. Ridership in 1992 exceeded 100,000. The railroad has the coach capacity to bring as many as 368,000 people a year to the rim, not only from Williams but also from the airport terminal and nearby auto parking areas. These figures suggest that use of the trains to the rim would significantly reduce vehicle congestion and pollution.

Edward Abbey's words about the Canyon and its history offer a fitting closure to this segment of Canyon history. In 1986, shortly before his untimely death, he wrote that it is not enough

> to describe the world of nature; the point is to preserve it. It is not enough to paint, photograph, or even to understand the American West; the point is to save it. . . . What we need are heroes and heroines—about a million of them—willing and able to fight for the health of the land and its native inhabitants.

J. B. Priestly, whose visit to the Canyon is described earlier, penned similar thoughts about the beauty to be protected at the Canyon. He wrote in 1937:

> What a possession for a country! And let me add how well the country looks after it. The American does not boast enough about his National Parks. Their very existence is something to boast about. The finest pieces of landscape in North America, perhaps in the world, belong to the People and are theirs to enjoy.

Such was exactly the attitude of Mary Jane Colter and many environmentalists like her. Part of that goal is realized by the continuing saga of the Grand Canyon line, which offers environmental protection to the Canyon along with its historic and archeological gifts.

www.ingramcontent.com/pod-product-compliance
Lightning Source LLC
Chambersburg PA
CBHW022306060426
42446CB00007BA/607